CULTURES OF THE WORLD
Kazakhstan

Cavendish
Square
New York

Published in 2020 by Cavendish Square Publishing, LLC
243 5th Avenue, Suite 136, New York, NY 10016

Library of Congress Cataloging-in-Publication Data

Names: Pang, Guek-Cheng, 1950- author. | Bryan, Bethany, author.
Title: Kazakhstan / Guek-Cheng Pang and Bethany Bryan.
Description: Third edition. | New York : Cavendish Square Publishing, 2020.
  | Series: Cultures of the world | Includes bibliographical references
  and index.
Identifiers: LCCN 2019055977 (print) | LCCN 2019055978 (ebook) | ISBN
  9781502655790 (library binding) | ISBN 9781502655806 (ebook)
Subjects: LCSH: Kazakhstan--Juvenile literature.
Classification: LCC DK903 .C49 2020 (print) | LCC DK903 (ebook) | DDC
  958.45--dc23
LC record available at https://lccn.loc.gov/2019055977
LC ebook record available at https://lccn.loc.gov/2019055978

Editor: Kristen Susienka
Copy Editor: Nathan Heidelberger
Designer: Jessica Nevins

Find us on

CONTENTS

KAZAKHSTAN TODAY

THE NAME "KAZAKHSTAN" COMES FROM THE WORD *KAZ*, A TURKIC word that means "to wander," and the Persian word *stan*, which means "place or land of." Kazakhstan is, therefore, a "land of wanderers." It is a region that united a people of nomadic, or wandering, tribes. They dealt with invasions from outside attackers and integrated, or mixed, with former enemies to form new tribes. In the late 15th century, the peoples finally joined together under the name Kazakhs—a group of free wanderers.

LOSS OF INDEPENDENCE

The united Kazakhs were under constant threat. They were in a precarious, or delicate, location, between Russia and China, and amid groups of invading Mongols. By 1822, they accepted protection from Russia, giving the larger country some control of their lands in exchange. This act would eventually take away the "free-wandering" lifestyle that Kazakhs had enjoyed for centuries. The Bolshevik uprising of 1917 turned Russia into the Union of Soviet Socialist Republics (USSR), which sought to industrialize

Kazakhstan and tame its wild and free-roaming people. In 1936, Kazakhstan would officially become a full republic of the USSR. Many Kazakhs fled the oppressive Soviet regime and the famine that resulted as a traditionally nomadic people saw their herds seized and were forced to farm the dry steppe regions of Soviet Kazakhstan. The ones who stayed saw their culture surrender to communism and their traditions all but disappear. For the next several decades, the idea of an independent Kazakhstan faded away for many Kazakhs. In 1991, however, the Soviet Union collapsed, and Kazakhstan finally declared itself an independent nation.

Free from Communist Party rule, many Kazakhs can again embrace the nomadic lifestyle that shaped their culture.

TODAY'S INDEPENDENT KAZAKHSTAN

Today, Kazakhstan is a nation that continues to struggle with its identity. During Soviet rule, Kazakhs adapted to the principles of communism. They adopted elements of Russian culture, like food and literature. They became used to giving up the things that made them proud Kazakhs.

As an independent state, Kazakhstan is finally seeing many of its people return, after years of living in countries like China and Mongolia. It's pushing aside Russian influences, making sweeping changes to language, architectural styles, and even the currency, to put the Kazakh Soviet Socialist Republic in its past. Kazakhs are hoping that these changes will establish a sense of independence from Russia once and for all, and pave the way to a bright future.

One of the biggest steps forward that Kazakhstan has taken is in its economy. Kazakhstan is rich with fossil fuels like crude oil and natural gas. This makes it stand out among the rest of the countries in Central Asia. Its location between China and Russia now makes it an ideal and powerful trading partner—and Kazakhstan is ready to trade. The economy is booming, with the gross domestic product (GDP), or total value of goods and services produced within the country, steadily rising year after year. This healthy economy has given Kazakhstan some ability to partner with international investors on expanding its infrastructure, building roads, pipelines, and railroads that reduce its reliance on Russia for help transporting goods out of the landlocked nation.

In the 21st century, business is booming for Kazakh architects, designers, and engineers as cities are growing and as structures built while the country was under Soviet rule are being replaced. Kazakhs are moving to cities in droves. Government officials are also aware that an economy dependent on finite natural resources isn't necessarily a stable one, so the government is beginning to invest in green, or environmentally conscious, and sustainable technologies. They're also working to reverse some of the damage caused by nuclear testing and the coal industry in decades past.

GOVERNMENT SHIFTS

Big changes are happening within the government's leadership as well. Longtime president Nursultan Nazarbayev, who came to power before Kazakhstan was an independent nation, stepped down in March 2019 after 29 years. He was replaced by Kassym-Jomart Tokayev, who Nazarbayev had chosen as his successor, although his role as president wasn't official until elections took place in June 2019. As president, Nazarbayev ushered Kazakhstan into a new era, working through the economic hardship of the early stages

A citizen is restrained just a few days before the general election in 2019, during protests demanding improvements to social benefits and housing for poor families.

of independence and helping to construct a government, a constitution, and a long-term plan for success. While he was no doubt influential, many feel that his departure is another step toward putting communism firmly in Kazakhstan's past.

YOUTH IN REVOLT

As of 2019, over half of Kazakhstan's population was 29 years of age or younger. This generation grew up in post-communist Kazakhstan and the internet age, and many know that if they are dissatisfied with their government, they can effect change through protest because they have seen it happen in other countries. In September 2019, 57 protesters were arrested during a demonstration against Chinese expansion into the oil and gas industries in Kazakhstan. Protesters believe that Chinese companies hire fewer Kazakhs and pay them less than foreign employees. Demonstrations also dominated the news around Nazarbayev's retirement and the election to replace him.

Not only are they speaking out politically, but younger Kazakhs are actively learning to embrace their history, reclaiming ancestral culture: music, dance, language, food, and the freedom to ride across the steppes with a herd of horses. This reclamation of their history influences modern ideas. Modern art, theater, dance, and pop music are becoming mainstays in Kazakhstan, with influences from the past as a popular theme.

Kazakhstan is a country where the past meets the present, where history and modernism converge. It's made up of vasts swatches of land and natural resources. It's a work in progress, with a bright future ahead.

GEOGRAPHY

Nomad yurts, traditional dwellings that are like tents, sit at the base of a mountain in the steppes of Kazakhstan.

AT ALMOST FOUR TIMES THE SIZE OF Texas, the nation of Kazakhstan is the ninth-largest country in the world. Covering 1,052,090 square miles (2,724,900 square kilometers), this landlocked nation borders Russia, China, Kyrgyzstan, Turkmenistan, and Uzbekistan.

From north to south, it measures about 1,025 miles (1,650 km) at its widest point, stretching from Russia in the north to Uzbekistan in the south. Meanwhile, it spans about 1,800 miles (2,900 km) from its western border with Russia to its eastern border with China. Its easternmost point is only about 25 miles (40 km) away from the western tip of Mongolia, though the two countries do not touch.

Kazakhstan used to be a part of the Soviet Union before its breakup in 1991. Today, Kazakhstan's population of 18,744,548 people makes it the third most populous republic in the Commonwealth of Independent States (CIS), which also includes Armenia, Azerbaijan, Belarus, Kyrgyzstan, Moldova, the Russian Federation, Tajikistan, Turkmenistan, and Uzbekistan.

A DIVERSE LANDSCAPE

Kazakhstan is mostly desert, but small portions of mixed prairie and forest or treeless prairie also exist. Mountainous regions also transform the landscape at times. The Tien Shan mountain chain, lying along the border of Kazakhstan, Kyrgyzstan, and China, rises mightily in the southeast. The Altai (or Altay) mountain system, with three distinctive ridges, is in the northeast. Also in the east is Lake Balkhash, a huge, shallow pool that

"For those who like their solitude, there are few places quite as expansive and lonesome as the steppes of Kazakhstan."
—The *Independent* newspaper, 2008

RUSSIA

RUSSIA

MONG.

Petropavl

Kostanay

Pavlodar

Uralsk

NUR-SULTAN ●

Semey

Oskemen

Aktobe

Karaganda

Atyrau

KAZAKHSTAN

Lake Balkhash

Aral Sea

CHINA

Aktau

Baykonur

Kyzylorda

Caspian
Sea

Almaty

AZER.

Taraz

UZBEKISTAN

Shymkent

KYRGYZSTAN

TURKMENISTAN

Landlocked
Kazakhstan is
bordered by the
equally landlocked
Caspian Sea, the
world's largest
body of water of
its type.

is distinctive because the eastern half is salty while the western half consists of fresh water. Farther inland are the Chingiz-Tau Mountains, rising to about 5,000 feet (1,525 meters). The Caspian Depression, a dominant feature in the west and southwest, is as much as 95 feet (29 m) below sea level at its lowest point. South of the depression are the Ustyurt Plateau and Tupqaraghan Peninsula, which borders the Caspian Sea. The Greater Barsuki Desert and the Kyzylkum Desert are located near the Aral Sea, while the Muyunkum Desert and the Betpaqdala Desert lie in south-central Kazakhstan.

FERTILE LANDS AND RESOURCES

In the north, the landscape is a mixture of forests and steppe. This is the most fertile region in the country, although the soil system is very fragile. It is also the most heavily cultivated and most agriculturally productive region. As one travels south, the grasslands change to desert and semidesert areas. Unsuitable for agriculture, the deserts are vast, empty, and desolate, and little has changed since the days when Genghis Khan and his Mongol hordes swept through Central Asia. However, underneath this apparent wasteland are

>

THE CASPIAN SEA

While Kazakhstan is a landlocked nation, one that has no ocean coastline or seaport, it does border the Caspian Sea, a large body of water that is itself landlocked. The Caspian Sea is a remnant of the ancient Tethys Ocean, which connected the Atlantic and Pacific Oceans between 50 and 60 million years ago. As continents shifted, much of the Tethys Ocean evaporated. Its origins as part of a long-gone ocean are why the Caspian Sea remains salty today. There are several islands in the Caspian Sea, but most of them do not have people living on them.

reserves of oil, gas, and rich mineral resources. Despite this, Kazakhstan's oil and gas industry, upon which much of the country's economy relies, is concentrated in the Caspian Sea region, where refineries are prevalent.

MOUNTAIN RANGES

In the east and southeast, the rich lowlands give way to hills and foothills, eventually rising to the Tien Shan and Altai mountain ranges that Kazakhstan shares with its neighbors. Kazakhstan's most beautiful scenery can be found in this region.

The Tien Shan Mountains stretch for 1,500 miles (2,400 km), straddling the borders of China, Kyrgyzstan, and Kazakhstan.

The Tien Shan Mountains (the name means "Heavenly Mountains" in Chinese) are the major mountain system in Central Asia. They stretch over 1,500 miles (2,400 km), through China, Kyrgyzstan, and Kazakhstan. The highest point in Kazakhstan, the 22,949-foot (6,995 m) Khan-Tengri Peak, is located in the Tien Shan range, but it is not the highest peak in these mountains. That is Pobedy Peak—Russian for "victory"—which rises to 24,406 feet (7,439 m) in eastern Kyrgyzstan. The Altai Mountains are a gentle range, with more woods and meadows than rocks and ravines.

BODIES OF WATER

Many of Kazakhstan's rivers have their source in these mountain ranges. Except for the Tobol (Tobyl in Kazakh), Ishim (Esil), and Irtysh (Ertis) Rivers that flow into the Arctic Ocean after joining the Ob River in Russia, the rest of the rivers flow into the Caspian and Aral Seas or disappear into the deserts and steppes. Many of the 7,000 streams are seasonal and evaporate in the summer.

There are three major river systems in this country. In the west, the Ural and Emba Rivers flow through the Caspian Depression before ending their journey in the Caspian Sea. In the southeast, several rivers flow out of the highlands. Of these, the largest rivers are the Chu and the Syr Darya. The Chu ends in the Muyunkum Desert and the Betpaqdala Basin. The Syr Darya empties into the Aral Sea. The third system flows from the Tien Shan Mountains into Lake Balkhash. The Ili and Ayaguz Rivers are the largest in this system. Many of Kazakhstan's rivers are glacier-fed, or gain water as glaciers retreat during the summer months. However, today the Tuyuksu Glacier in the Tien Shan Mountains is losing more and more of its ice mass each year because of global warming. This results in less water filtering into the rivers. Scientists are keeping a close eye on these changes, since so much of Kazakhstan relies on glacier-fed streams and rivers for drinking water and crop irrigation. Without them, effects could be deadly.

Kazakhstan has more than 48,000 lakes, but most of these have an area of less than 1 square mile (2.6 sq km). Those in the lowlands and the deserts are usually salty lakes, while those in the north and in the mountains are fed with fresh water from the snow. The Caspian and Aral Seas and Lake Balkhash are the three largest bodies of water in the country.

WEATHER AND CLIMATE

A landlocked country located at a great distance from the sea, Kazakhstan has a continental climate. This means it is affected by the large landmasses surrounding it rather than by oceans. It is very cold in the winter, especially in the north, where temperatures can drop to −58 degrees Fahrenheit (−50 degrees Celsius). In the summer, especially in the southern deserts, it can be as hot as 113°F (45°C).

Kazakhstan is also a dry country, especially in the south-central region, which receives only about 4 inches (10 centimeters) of rain annually. The country is so far inland that moisture-laden ocean winds drop their rainwater

> ## THE GOLDEN EAGLE
>
> *The golden eagle is one of Kazakhstan's national symbols and appears on the national flag. Kazakhs consider the eagle a symbol of power and strength because it is the master of the skies. The female bird is larger than the male, measuring 3 feet (1 m) from beak to tail. The eagle has a wingspan of 7.5 feet (2.3 m). Its overall color is dark brown, but the feathers over the back of the head and neck are a distinct golden color, hence its name. Golden eagles nest in high, mountainous areas on cliff ledges and in the tops of tall trees. They can also be found in the mountainous regions of the United States, Canada, and Mexico.*

long before they reach Kazakhstan. The lack of rain means that most days are sunny, and the skies are often blue and cloudless. The wettest part of the country is in the mountainous eastern region, which gets as much as 24 inches (61 cm) of precipitation a year, mainly in the form of snow.

PLANTS AND ANIMALS

Kazakhstan is rich in flora and fauna. Several nature reserves have been established to try to protect the uniqueness of the land, the most recent being the Ile-Balkhash State Nature Reserve in July 2018. There are more than 6,000 species of plants, of which 535 are found only in Kazakhstan. About 155 species of mammals, over 500 species of birds, and 150 species of fish add to the diversity.

The country has few forests; it is mostly grassland, with dry shrubby wormwood, Russian thistle, black saxaul, and tamarisk growing on the plains and in the deserts, and feather grass growing on the drier plains. Naurzum Nature Reserve in the Kostanay region was established in 1931 to protect the pine forests there. The area shelters several rare animals, such as the mouflon, a kind of wild sheep; the long-needled hedgehog; wildcats such as the caracal and barkhan, or sand cat; and the beautiful bustard, a game bird.

The Tien Shan Mountains are home to the endangered snow leopard; Tien Shan brown bear; Siberian stag; bearded vulture, with a wingspan of over

The Naurzum Nature Reserve protects a number of plant and animal species, including certain species of pine tree, wolves, and hedgehogs.

10 feet (3 m); Himalayan ular, or mountain turkey-hen; and golden eagle. In the Altai Mountains, the giant Siberian stag and the small musk deer can be found. Lake Alakol in the southeast is a nature reserve and is the habitat for rare birds such as the fish hawk and the black stork.

The fresh and saltwater lakes of the steppes attract all kinds of migrating birds. In addition, there are numerous species of ducks, geese, herons, gulls, sandpipers, and terns. Lake Tengiz in central Kazakhstan attracts millions of migratory birds every year and hosts the northernmost nesting colony of pink flamingos. Birds of prey—eagles, merlins, kestrels, and others—circle the skies. Large herds of saiga antelope and elk roam the plains.

The deserts are home to hordes of gazelles. There are also many species of jerboas, polecats, and birds such as the jay, lark, and desert dove. One of the world's largest lizards, the gray monitor lizard, lives in the Kyzylkum Desert. There are many other species of lizards and snakes.

Fishermen catch sturgeon, trout, carp, herring, and roach in the seas, rivers, and lakes. The sheatfish, a type of catfish that can grow to more than 6.6 feet (2 m) long and weigh more than 440 pounds (200 kilograms), is a game fish sought by anglers fishing in the Ili River system.

SMALL TOWNS AND LARGE CITIES

Before the 20th century, Kazakhstan had few large cities. The Kazakhs were nomads and lived in yurts, which are tent-like structures, or in small villages that centered on farming or that were located on trade routes. After World War II, an influx of Russian industrial workers resulted in a rapid growth of cities. Now, over 57 percent of the population lives in cities.

In 1997, President Nursultan Nazarbayev moved the capital city of Kazakhstan from Almaty to Akmola, renaming the new capital city Astana. Over the next few decades, the city was built up and expanded. Japanese architect Kurokawa Kisho was brought in to design streets and buildings, including a brand-new Presidential Palace, or home of the president. The city's name was changed again in 2019 to Nur-Sultan, in honor of the long-serving president as he left office.

The towns are small settlements or villages separated by large areas of cultivated land in the north or inhospitable plains and deserts in the south. Typical Soviet-planned towns, such as Karaganda and Oskemen, have straight, wide streets that are bordered by nondescript gray buildings several stories high and surrounded by industrial zones.

NUR-SULTAN   The town of Akmola was made the capital of the country in 1997 and renamed Astana (which means "capital" in Kazakh) the following year by a decree of the president of the republic, Nursultan Nazarbayev. When Nazarbayev left office in 2019, the city's name changed again in his honor, becoming Nur-Sultan.

Changing the name of the city is not a new occurrence. It was known as Akmolinsk before becoming Tselinograd in 1961, and then Akmola in 1992. It is at the junction of the Trans-Kazakhstan and South Siberian Railroads, along the banks of the Ishim (Esil) River in the north-central part of the country. The town was originally a Russian military outpost in the 19th century and later became an administrative center for the region. It became particularly important in the 1950s, when the Soviet Union adopted a Virgin Lands policy. This move billed the land of Kazakhstan as untouched, perfect for building. It forced people from Ukraine and other areas of the USSR to move to the country's steppe regions in an attempt to create successful farms there. However, the land was too dry, and adequate farming was difficult. More activity occurred in this city, however. There was a tremendous amount of building activity, and several research and educational institutions were

"Little surrounds the city (of Nur-Sultan) for 1,200 kilometers (750 miles), save a handful of provincial towns dotted across the world's largest steppe, a flat, empty expanse of grassland."
—Daisy Carrington, writer/producer for CNN

Almaty is the
largest and most
populous city
in Kazakhstan,
located in the
southern region.

established in the city. Today, there are metal-finishing factories there that process copper, gold, and bauxite from mines in the region. There has been a big population influx into the city, even though it is not the biggest city in Kazakhstan. Most of the townspeople work on the railroad and in factories. The population of Nur-Sultan was 602,480 in 2007, growing to over 1 million by 2019.

ALMATY   With over 1.8 million inhabitants, Almaty is the largest city in Kazakhstan. It was named after the apple trees for which it is famous. In 1854, the Russians established a frontier post in Almaty and called it Vernyi. Soon after a fort was established, Cossacks and Siberian peasant farmers settled in the area. The city was devastated by two earthquakes in 1887 and 1911. In 1921, the Soviets changed the name of the city to Alma-Ata, meaning "father of apples." In 1929, Alma-Ata became the capital of Soviet Kazakhstan. In 1992, the city's name changed again to Almaty.

The city is an orderly grid pattern of roads that slope from south to north. It is the financial, industrial, culinary, and educational center of the country. Its citizens are service sector workers and industrial workers in the country's bustling manufacturing industries. Since independence, Almaty has developed an air of cosmopolitanism and a spirit of adventure. Many visitors come here in search of opportunities—Chinese Uighur traders from Urumchi, in Xinjiang, sell their wares in the bazaar, while Western businesspeople hope to finalize some business deals. The city also is home to cultural enjoyments such as a zoo, a botanical garden, an opera house, and theaters.

SHYMKENT The city of Shymkent (Chimkent is the Russian spelling) in the south lies along the route of the Turkestan-Siberia Railroad. It was founded in the 12th century on the strength of trade between the nomads and the citizens of Kokand in Uzbekistan. However, this once pretty little town was completely destroyed by heavy Russian shelling in 1864. It has been rebuilt since World War II. In the past, the main industry was lead smelting from ore

The city of Shymkent was once dominated by the lead-mining industry, resulting in extreme pollution. Today, it is driven by cleaner manufacturing industries.

mined in the nearby Karatau Hills. The lead was used to make bullets. This industry resulted in severe air pollution, giving the city a reputation of being gray and dreary. Today, the chemical industry is pushing its way to the top of the city's economy. There are also cement works and fruit canneries. In 2019, the Kazakh government decided to invest around $3.3 billion to develop and upgrade the infrastructure of Shymkent by 2023.

TARAZ   Like other Kazakh cities, Taraz has undergone many name changes. It stands on the site of an old city built in the sixth century. It claims to have been a capital of the Turks in the 11th century, but this distinction is also claimed by the cities of Bukhara in Uzbekistan and Balasagun in Kyrgyzstan. It was an important stop along the famous Silk Road trading route but was practically destroyed by the Mongols in the 13th century. In 1864, it was captured by the Russians and renamed Aulie-Ata. When Kazakhstan became a republic in 1936, the city's name was changed again. It became Zhambyl, in honor of Zhambyl Zhabaev, a local folk singer. Finally, in 1992, it regained its old name of Taraz. The town has also undergone changes in appearance, from a majestic city of mosques and minarets to one filled with apartment blocks where industry has contributed to air pollution. Factories produce phosphate, sugar, leather, and footwear.

SEMEY   Located in northeastern Kazakhstan, near the Russian border, Semey is probably the most Russian-looking of Kazakh towns. It was founded near a Russian fort in 1718, not far from the ruins of a Buddhist monastery. Among the ruins were seven buildings, which inspired the region's name, Semipalatinsk, meaning "seven-halled." It moved to its current site in 1778 and became an important trading town in the late 19th century. Its most famous inhabitant was Fyodor Dostoevsky, the Russian author most well known for his work *Crime and Punishment*, who was exiled to this place between 1854 and 1859. Today, there is a museum, the F. M. Dostoevsky Literary and Memorial Museum, that includes the wooden house in which he lived. It tells of his life and the time he spent in Semipalatinsk. In more recent years, the town has become infamous for the secret nuclear testing done nearby beginning in 1949. Fortunately, this controversial practice ended in 1990, but not before statistics showed a higher-than-average incidence of cancer among its people. Semey, with a population of about 320,400, has food-processing, leather, textile, clothing, footwear, and lumber factories.

Since 2017, the five largest cities in Kazakhstan have begun to transform into smart cities under the leadership of the Kazakh government. This means the cities are becoming more technologically equipped. These changes will harness advanced technology to promote comfort, safety, efficiency, and sustainability for citizens and visitors. Updates include improved mapping, lighting, and traffic safety.

INTERNET LINKS

https://www.cnn.com/2012/07/13/world/asia/eye-on-kazakhstan-astana/index.html
This article offers beautiful photographs of some of the interesting, unique structures of Nur-Sultan, formerly Astana, the capital city of Kazakhstan.

https://ingeo.kz/?p=5877&lang=en
The website for the Institute of Geography of the Republic of Kazakhstan tracks some of the current issues affecting Kazakhstan's geography.

HISTORY

KAZAKHSTAN HAS ALWAYS BEEN A nation of nomads. Tens of thousands of years ago, the first modern *Homo sapiens* settled there, ancient Turkic tribes following the availability of food for their livestock and for themselves.

In the fifth century CE, the Huns, a nomadic Central Asian people, attacked the great Roman Empire under the fierce leadership of the warrior Attila. The Huns were succeeded by tribes of Turkic-speaking people who were organized into political units known as khanates. In the centuries that followed, several regions of Kazakhstan belonged to different empires. During the 13th century, most of it was part of the Mongol Empire. The Kazakhs, who were, in fact, Uzbeks who had grown dissatisfied with their khan, or ruler, did not arrive in Kazakhstan until the 15th century.

THE ARRIVAL OF GENGHIS KHAN

The earliest state that historians are aware of in the region was that of the Turkic Khanate, established in the sixth century CE. In the eighth century, the Kazakhstan region attracted the attention of the outside world because it lay along the Silk Road that connected Europe to China. This route passed near Almaty.

For the next few centuries, various parts of the region were dominated by confederations, or groups, of Turkic tribes and Arabs who brought the religion of Islam with them. They fought among themselves until Mongol

In August 2019, archaeologists excavating a cemetery in central Kazakhstan dating back to the Bronze Age uncovered the remains of a couple buried face to face and locked in an eternal embrace. Gold, jewelry, knives, and ceramic pots also found in the grave suggest that the couple might have been nobles. Archaeologists believe the couple may have been buried as far back as 2000 BCE.

armies invaded the area under the banner of Genghis Khan in the 13th century and imposed Mongol customs on the people.

After the Mongol invasion, the tribes in the area came under the control of a succession of khans of the western branch of the Mongol Empire, called the Golden Horde. The Golden Horde later split into smaller groups, including the Nogai Horde and the Uzbek Khanate.

INDEPENDENCE FOR KAZAKHS

The Kazakhs emerged as a recognizable group in the mid-15th century, when some of the tribes broke away from the khanates and sought independence.

The breakaway was led by Janybek and Kerey, two sons of the Barak Khan of the White Horde of the Mongol Empire. They led their people in a revolt against Abul Khayr of the Uzbek Khanate. Kazakhs believe this to be the beginning of their nation. Janybek and Kerey led their supporters to the land near the Chu River. As time went on, their supporters and the territory they controlled grew. Although they belonged to the Uzbek tribe, they were also called "Kazakhs" because the word meant a people who had wandered away and who were free and independent. The Kazakhs had a more nomadic lifestyle than the Uzbeks, who were more sedentary.

After Janybek and Kerey, the next great leader was Kasym Khan, who united the Kazakh tribes. During the late 15th century and throughout the 16th century, the Kazakhs were a strong, nomadic empire that ruled the steppes from the shores of the Caspian and Aral Seas in the south and west to the upper Irtysh (Ertis) River in the east. Kasym Khan was believed to have in his service more than 200,000 warrior horsemen who were feared by all their neighbors.

THE THREE HORDES

This unity, however, was short lived. During the successive reigns of Kasym Khan's three sons, the Kazakhs soon separated into three new tribal federations called the Great Horde, which controlled the southeastern region north of the Tien Shan Mountains; the Middle Horde, which ruled in the north-central region east of the Aral Sea; and the Lesser Horde, which occupied the west between the Aral Sea and the Ural River. The ruling khan held the ultimate authority in each horde, or khanate. However, his power was dependent upon that of the sultans, or tribal chiefs, and theirs upon the loyalty of the *biys* (BEES), who were the heads of the clans who made up the horde, and the *batyrs*, who were the warrior class.

The khans' rule is long over, but statues dedicated to their memory stand all over Kazakhstan.

This was the situation until the 17th century, when Russian traders and soldiers appeared on the scene. The Russians set up an outpost on the north coast of the Caspian Sea in 1645 and from then on built more forts and seized control of more and more Kazakh territory.

From the 1680s to the 1770s, the Kazakhs were at war with the Oyrat federation of four western Mongol tribes. The Russians gained increasing control because the Kazakhs were pressured from the east by the Mongols, forcing them westward. In 1730, Abul Khayr, the khan of the Lesser Horde, sought Russian help. This alliance unfortunately gave the Russians permanent control over the Lesser Horde. In 1732, part of the Middle Horde was incorporated by Russia. The Russians conquered the Middle Horde by 1798. The Great Horde managed to remain independent until the 1820s, when the expanding Qugen (Kokand) Khanate in the south forced them to choose Russian protection.

RUSSIAN CONTROL

Life on the steppes continued without too much interference from the Russians until the 1820s, when the Russians decided to introduce a new system of administration. The land was divided into administrative units that allowed the czarist government to tax the people, and Russian military rule was imposed.

The three khanates were abolished: the Middle Horde in 1822; the Lesser Horde in 1824; and the Great Horde in 1848.

The Kazakhs resisted Russian rule from the beginning. The first big revolt was led by Khan Kene (also known as Kenesary Kasymov) of the Middle Horde between 1837 and 1847. Despite Kazakh resistance, the Russians continued to colonize the land and built a series of forts. Khan Kene was killed in 1847 after a bitter struggle. He is seen as a Kazakh national hero.

The construction of Russian forts was the beginning of the end of the traditional life of the people by limiting the area over which animals could graze. When Russians settled the fertile lands of northern and eastern Kazakhstan in the 1890s, it signaled the complete destruction of nomadic life there. Then, between 1906 and 1912, more than half a million farms were established by the Russians. As increasing numbers of Russian and Ukrainian peasants arrived, the Kazakhs were forced to emigrate east to China.

When the Russian government tried to recruit the Kazakhs in 1916 to fight against Germany in World War I, the people, already starving and displaced from their lands, resisted conscription into the Russian Imperial Army. This resistance, led by Amangeldy Imanov, was brutally crushed. Thousands of Kazakhs were killed, while thousands of others fled to China and Mongolia. As a punishment, those nomads who had taken part in the revolt were driven from their lands, and the area was made available to Russian settlers.

In 1917, when news of the Russian Revolution and the collapse of imperial Russia reached Kazakhstan, the Kazakhs, led by their westernized intelligentsia, or educated elite, revolted again. Under the leadership of Alikhan Bukeikhanov, they set up a party called Alash Orda (Horde of Alash).

The Bolsheviks took over power in Russia in October 1917 and began to set up revolutionary committees and armed units in Kazakhstan. They allowed the Kazakhs to establish an independent state under the Alash Orda party. It only survived for a few years before being suppressed by the Soviets in 1920. The Kazakhs accepted Soviet rule, and some of the country's leaders joined the Communist Party. The period of Stalinist terror that began in the late 1920s, during which Joseph Stalin's government brutally controlled the Soviet people, was also the time when the Kazakh steppes became a part of the infamous Soviet "Gulag Archipelago." The government set up camps, called gulags, throughout Kazakhstan and other remote parts of the Soviet Union and deported intellectuals and other dissenters there. Among those who were exiled in Kazakhstan were Soviet literary theoretician Mikhail Bakhtin and writer Aleksandr Isayevich Solzhenitsyn, whose work *The Gulag Archipelago* documents the gulag system.

KAZAKHSTAN AS A SOVIET REPUBLIC

In 1936, Kazakhstan became a Soviet republic. During this period, the leaders of the republic were mostly non-locals rather than Kazakhs.

Joseph Stalin strong-armed, or forced, his way to leadership after Lenin's death. Many of his policies led to famine and the deaths of numerous Kazakhs.

From 1929 to 1937, Russian agriculture was collectivized under a policy launched by Soviet leader Joseph Stalin. The Kazakhs suffered because many peasants killed their livestock to protest this policy, and thousands later fled to China and Afghanistan. It is estimated that at least 1.5 million Kazakhs died during this time. In addition, famine killed more than 80 percent of the country's livestock.

The Soviets also discouraged nomadic life and encouraged permanent settlement. They pursued an antireligious policy, arresting religious leaders and anyone suspected of being a nationalist. All religious organizations were closed to force people to conform.

To develop the economy, the government promoted industrialization. As industry expanded, skilled workers immigrated to the country. During World War II, much of Russia's industry was moved to Kazakhstan to prevent its capture by the Germans.

WORLD WAR II RESETTLEMENTS

Various other peoples—Crimean Tatars, Volga Germans, Poles, Chechens, and Koreans—were resettled in the Kazakh region because the Russians distrusted them or were afraid that they would collaborate with Germany during World War II. Muslims from nearby countries, including those from Azerbaijan and Uighurs from China, also moved to Kazakhstan.

Between 1953 and 1965, the Soviet campaign to increase the production of wheat and other grains led to large areas of grazing land in the vast grasslands in northern Kazakhstan being put under the plow. This was due to the Virgin

Propaganda posters like this one gave those who were resettled the idea that prosperity awaited them in Kazakhstan.

and Idle Lands program. In 1954, Nikita Khrushchev, who was then first secretary of the Communist Party, sent his assistant Leonid Brezhnev as his representative to the Kazakh SSR (Soviet Socialist Republic) to supervise the Virgin and Idle Lands experiment. This program brought another influx of Russian and Ukrainian farmers to the region. After Brezhnev was recalled to Moscow, a Kazakh named Dinmukhamed Kunayev became first secretary of the Communist Party of Kazakhstan. However, as a result of the failure of the agricultural policies and other economic problems, Kunayev was forced to resign. He came back into power in 1964 and became the first Kazakh to become a full member of the ruling Politburo, or policymaking group, of the Soviet Union. As a leader of great foresight and achievement, Kunayev looked after the needs of Kazakhs and Russians with equal care.

KAZAKHSTAN'S FAILED ECONOMY

Kunayev initially raised the standard of living of his people and instituted reforms in higher education that allowed more people to attend college and get better jobs. He stayed in power for over 20 years before coming under attack for mismanagement, favoritism, and misconduct when the economy failed. In 1986, Soviet leader Mikhail Gorbachev forced him to resign. His dismissal caused unrest—many people took to the streets to demonstrate, producing one of the most serious riots in the Soviet Union in the 1980s.

Kunayev was replaced with an ethnic Russian, Gennady Kolbin. Many people were against Kolbin's appointment and rioted and held demonstrations. There are conflicting reports as to how many people were killed, injured, and arrested in this upset. Some reports say at least 200 people died and more than 1,000 were injured. Kolbin was an administrator who instituted economic and social reforms that were Soviet-inspired and unrealistic, causing the economy to deteriorate further. Agricultural output continued to drop, hitting such a low point in 1989 that Kolbin suggested killing wild ducks that were migrating through the country to provide meat for the people.

KHRUSHCHEV'S NEW POLICY

Under Nikita Khrushchev, who was the Soviet premier, or leader, from 1958 to 1964, large areas of virgin, or previously uncultivated, land in the Ural Mountains, Siberia, and Kazakhstan were opened to farming. The aim was to reduce the import of grain into Central Asia and to encourage the nomadic people to adopt a more settled way of life. Under the program, about 60 percent of Kazakhstan's pastureland was cultivated. Unfortunately, there were several things wrong with the program. It was unrealistically based on forecasts of grain production from years of high yield. Thus, actual production figures fell short of what was expected. Other problems included a climate and soil conditions that were not suited to agriculture, a poor choice of crops, and a lack of equipment and labor. After several years of crop failures and other problems, Khrushchev was ousted from his position as premier in 1964.

NATIONALISM IN KAZAKHSTAN

The late 1980s was a time of tremendous turmoil in the Soviet Union, which was facing imminent breakup. Mikhail Gorbachev attempted to hold the union together by calling for the election of a national legislature and a loosening of Soviet political control over the republics.

Starting in 1989, conflicts developed between the central parliament of the USSR and the parliaments of the individual republics, mainly over the respective powers that each should have. There were increasing demands in the republics for autonomy and even for full independence. At the Congress of People's Deputies in Moscow in June 1989, many informal political groups presented their nationalist programs. This feeling of nationalism was also echoed in Kazakhstan.

In June 1989, Kolbin returned to Moscow and was replaced by Nursultan Nazarbayev. In March 1990, elections were held. A new legislature consisting of a majority of ethnic Kazakhs and a minority of Russians was formed.

INDEPENDENCE

Nazarbayev, a Kazakh trained as a metallurgist and an engineer, proved himself to be a skilled politician. He became a member of the Communist Party in 1979 and

Russian president Boris Yeltsin (*second from right*) and Kazakhstan's president Nursultan Nazarbayev (*second from left*) can be seen here around the time of the dissolution of the USSR in 1991.

was made chairman of Kazakhstan's Council of Ministers in 1984. When Kunayev fell out of favor, Nazarbayev took on a major role in the attacks against Kunayev. Although he was passed over in favor of Kolbin in 1986, Nazarbayev was a strong supporter of Mikhail Gorbachev and his reform programs. He realized the importance of balancing Moscow's demands with increasing Kazakh nationalism. After he took over, he made Kazakh the official language, allowed for greater religious tolerance, and permitted criticism and an examination of the negative effects that collectivization and other Soviet policies had on the country.

Nazarbayev supported Gorbachev and the Soviet Union because he believed that the member republics were too economically dependent on each other to be able to survive on their own. However, he was also aware of the importance of gaining control of the country's mineral wealth. In June 1991, at his insistence, Moscow surrendered control of the mineral resources in Kazakhstan.

In September 1991, the three republics of Estonia, Latvia, and Lithuania achieved complete independence and were recognized as sovereign, or stand-alone, states. Several other republics were demanding independence. Gorbachev tried to establish a new "union of sovereign states" that would have some common foreign, defense, and economic policies, but no agreement could be reached with the remaining republics.

On December 16, 1991, Kazakhstan declared independence. On December 21, 1991, 12 of the 15 republics, including Kazakhstan, signed documents for the dissolution of the Soviet Union and the establishment of the Commonwealth of Independent States (CIS) that would share a common policy for foreign affairs and defense.

Nazarbayev, who remained in power until 2019, steered a careful course for his country. Kazakhstan remained heavily dependent upon Russia while working to establish its own independence once and for all. In 2017, Nazarbayev called for a big change to the Kazakh language that would help to set Kazakhstan apart from Russia: its own Latin alphabet. The language was updated twice in the space of one year. By 2025, the vision is that the Kazakh language will fully adopt the Latin alphabet, retiring the Cyrillic alphabet adopted from the Russian language and used for centuries.

A NEW LEADER

In March 2019, longtime Kazakhstan president Nursultan Nazarbayev, then 78 years old, announced that he would be stepping aside as president, though he would maintain an advisory role within the government. Nazarbayev's resignation effectively handed over power to the leader of the Senate, Kassym-Jomart Tokayev, who went on to win over 70 percent of the country's votes in the June 2019 general election. This transition of power was controversial, resulting in protests as Kazakh citizens spoke out against the undemocratic nature of the election, which many believed had been rigged in favor of Nazarbayev's choice of successor. These weren't the first government protests in recent times either. Demonstrations against a new land law spread throughout the country in 2016, and antigovernment protests have become regular occurrences ever since. As Kazakhstan continues to emerge from its restrictive Soviet past and its decades of rule by a single leader, such public displays of frustration will likely continue to be a mainstay of Kazakh society.

"There was no such thing as Kazakhstan. It was just a chunk of (the) Soviet Union. I had to build a country, to establish an army, our own police, our internal life, everything from roads to the constitution."
—Nursultan Nazarbayev

INTERNET LINKS

http://factsanddetails.com/central-asia/Kazakhstan/sub8_4a/entry-4633.html
This website offers a detailed breakdown of Kazakhstan declaring and achieving independence from the USSR.

http://news.bbc.co.uk/2/hi/asia-pacific/country_profiles/1298395.stm
This handy timeline offers a look at some key events from Kazakhstan's history.

https://www.nytimes.com/2019/06/09/world/asia/kazakhstan-election-president.html
Here you can read about protests that took place during the general election in Kazakhstan in 2019.

GOVERNMENT

This is the main residence of Kazakhstan's president.

3

F OR ALMOST 300 YEARS, Kazakhstan was in the control of Russia, and then the Soviet Union. In 1991, Kazakhstan declared its independence as the USSR dissolved into history. Nursultan Nazarbayev would become the first president of the nation of Kazakhstan, remaining in power for almost 30 years. Despite Kazakhstan being its own country, many of its leaders and ideas first developed while it was under Communist Party control. Today, Kazakhstan's government is facing a new era following the stepping down of Nazarbayev and other advances in leadership that are taking place.

"For centuries we have been living in the society where not laws but people ruled, where there was no legal state."
—Nursultan Nazarbayev

THE CONSTITUTION OF KAZAKHSTAN

The post-independence government of Kazakhstan consists of: the president, who is the head of government; an executive branch, represented by the Council of Ministers; a legislative branch made of the two houses of Parliament; and the judicial branch.

A NEW DIRECTION FOR KAZAKHSTAN?

Former president Nursultan Nazarbayev was in power for almost 30 years, stepping aside in 2019 but not surrendering all of his power as the presidency passed to Kassym-Jomart Tokayev. In a nation like Kazakhstan, where many citizens have only known one ruler for their entire lives, and where election results often feel outside of their control, there can be a fear of rocking the boat. Many also feel like their votes won't really matter in a country where, in 2011, Nazarbayev won 95.5 percent of the vote. With a new president in office, Kazakhstan is a nation whose future is up in the air. Kazakhstan may continue down a familiar path with leaders who refuse to step aside. However, as protesters continue to speak out against autocracy, there is a chance that the government will begin to listen.

Kazakhstan's constitution was last amended in 2017. Here, Nazarbayev speaks to the amendment committee.

Two new constitutions, written in 1993 and 1995, have ensured the power of the president and his control over various aspects of the government.

The 1993 constitution replaced the Soviet constitution, in force since 1978. Under this constitution, the prime minister and the Council of Ministers answered to the president. A new constitution in 1995 reinforced this relationship and placed the country under direct presidential rule. The constitution was drawn up by President Nazarbayev and his Council of Ministers. It was adopted by popular referendum on August 30, 1995. This constitution also established the principle of equal rights for people of all nationalities and made Kazakh and Russian the country's official languages.

Under the constitution, the president is the head of state. He is elected for a maximum of two consecutive, five-year terms, although this rule was not enforced in the case of Nazarbayev. In fact, in 2007, an amendment to the constitution made Nazarbayev exempt from the two-term rule. The president governs with the help of the Council of Ministers, whose key members he appoints. The head of the council is the prime minister. The president appoints the prime minister, as well as the chairperson of the National Security Committee. The president also has the authority to issue decrees and overrule actions taken by the ministries. There have been four rounds of amendments to

Kazakhstan's constitution. The latest changes were signed into law in 2017 by President Nazarbayev. In theory, they distributed some of the powers previously held by the president to other government officials, including more parliamentary oversight over the selection of ministers.

THE HOUSES OF PARLIAMENT

Parliament, as established by the 1995 constitution, is made up of two houses, the Senate and the Assembly, or Mazhilis. There are 49 seats in the Senate and 107 members of the Mazhilis, of which 98 are directly elected by the people. Members of the Senate serve six-year terms, with one-half of the membership renewed every three years, while terms in the Mazhilis last for five years.

These buildings in the capital city of Nur-Sultan house Kazakhstan's Parliament, including the 49-member Senate and the 107-member Mazhilis.

All members of Parliament must be Kazakh citizens who have been living in the country for at least 10 years. A person wishing to run for the Senate must be 30 years or older, must have had higher education and previous government service, and must have lived in the territory he or she wishes to represent for no less than three years. A member of the Mazhilis must be at least 25 years old. All Kazakh citizens ages 18 years and above are eligible to vote.

Members of the Senate and Mazhilis deal with the making of laws and their reform, the economy and the budget, international affairs, defense and security, regional development, and local administration.

POLITICAL PARTIES

Although former president Nazarbayev did not encourage a democratic society during his time as president, he balanced his authoritarian rule with some degree of allowance for opposition. Other parties besides Nazarbayev's hold seats in Parliament, but they are all friendly to the majority party and are not considered equal players in Kazakhstan's government. The only true opposition party in Kazakhstan is the National Social Democratic Party (NSDP). However, it did not win any seats in the Mazhilis in the 2016 election (the most recent), and it refused to participate in the presidential election of 2019 to protest what it saw as an unfair process.

Kazakhstan is divided into 14 provinces, plus three cities—Almaty, the former capital; Nur-Sultan, the current capital; and Shymkent. These cities have a special administrative status that is equal to a province. Baykonur (formerly called Leninsk), the site of the Soviet Union's space launch facility, also has special administrative status in that Kazakhstan has leased the area to Russia until 2050. Russia continues to operate a space facility there.

Each province is subdivided into regions and smaller administrative units of settlements. Every province has its own council responsible for budget, tax, and other administrative matters. The heads of local administration, known as akim *(a-KEEM), are appointed by the president and can only be removed from office by a two-thirds majority vote of no confidence by the local councils.*

Shown here is the party headquarters of the Nur Otan.

The political change that Kazakhstan has undergone since independence has led to a proliferation of social organizations, political parties, and special interest groups. There are 11 officially registered political parties that have formed, reformed, split, and combined. During the 2016 elections in Kazakhstan, candidates from six political parties ran for office. As of 2019, Nur Otan, or the Democratic People's Party, the ruling party of Kazakhstan, held 84 of the 98 directly elected seats in the Mazhilis. The Ak Zhol Democratic Party held 7 seats, and the last 7 seats were held by the Communist People's Party of Kazakhstan. To form a political group, several criteria are needed. First, there must be 40,000 members in the group to constitute it as valid. A group cannot be related to a religious denomination or based on ethnic origin or gender alone. There are also rules against "extremist" parties forming, but the definition of such remains vague.

THE JUDICIAL SYSTEM

Justice is served in Kazakhstan by the Supreme Court and local courts around the country. Small local courts hear cases of petty crime, such as vandalism, while provincial courts deal with bigger crimes, such as murders. Cases of

The Assembly of the People of Kazakhstan is a consultative and advisory body under the president. Its tasks include the promotion and maintenance of ethnic and social stability and the selection of the nine members of the Mazhilis that aren't directly elected by the Kazakh people. It makes policies and finds solutions for any social and cultural conflicts in Kazakh society. The assembly was established in 1995 by President Nazarbayev to help balance multilateral ethnic interests and address conflicts between Kazakh nationalist interests and Slavic insecurities. The president acts as chairman of the assembly and convenes the assembly at his own initiative or when asked to do so by at least a third of the assembly members. The members are made up of candidates sent by smaller assemblies in each region of the country.

appeal are sent to the Supreme Court of the Republic. The judicial branch also includes a Constitutional Council made up of a chairperson and six members who serve six-year terms of office. Today, there are 44 judges in the Supreme Court, all appointed by the president with approval of the Senate.

Of the six Constitutional Council judges, two are nominated by the president, two by the head of the Senate, and two by the head of the Mazhilis. The chairperson of the council is appointed by the president and is very powerful because he or she has the deciding vote if the council members are deadlocked over a case. In addition to these seven members, the 1995 constitution also makes all former presidents of the republic automatic members of the council for life.

Council members may not be members of Parliament, nor can they hold other employment except for some teaching, scientific, or creative activity. They may not be engaged in any private business or sit on an advisory council of a commercial enterprise.

It is the responsibility of the Constitutional Council to settle disputes about presidential and general elections, as well as those among parliamentary deputies. Besides ensuring that the laws to be adopted conform to the constitution, the council has to interpret the constitution and resolve all matters regarding constitutional procedures.

THE LEADERS OF KAZAKHSTAN

As of early 2020, the president of Kazakhstan is Kassym-Jomart Tokayev. Tokayev served as the deputy foreign minister of Kazakhstan starting in 1992. He was appointed prime minister in 1999 and became state secretary in 2002. He served as the minister of foreign affairs from 2003 to 2007. Immediately before becoming president, he was serving as leader of the Senate. Although Tokayev is president, as of 2020, former president Nursultan Nazarbayev holds many responsibilities in Kazakhstan's government, especially in foreign affairs, since he maintains relationships with many world leaders like Russia's Vladimir Putin and China's Xi Jinping.

The prime minister is Askar Mamin, appointed in 2019 by Nazarbayev. Mamin was formerly the first deputy prime minister and former mayor of Astana (now Nur-Sultan).

The first deputy prime minister is Alikhan Smailov. He had previously served as Kazakhstan's minister of finance.

MILITARY FORCE

Kazakh soldiers participate in a military parade in 2018.

When Kazakhstan became independent in 1991, it had no military force because its defense and security matters had been taken care of by the Soviet army. A Kazakh military force was established in 1992 when the former Soviet 40th Army, stationed on Kazakh soil, was nationalized. Kazakhstan now has three branches within the Kazakhstan Armed Forces: Land Forces, Navy, and Air Defense Force. All male citizens between the ages of 18 and 27 are required to serve in the military for at least one year.

FOREIGN RELATIONS

Despite the breakup of the Soviet Union, Kazakhstan's ties with the former members of the union are still strong, and there are bilateral trade and security agreements with these countries. In 1994, Kazakhstan, Uzbekistan, and Kyrgyzstan set up a free-trade zone. Kazakhstan also tries to play a part in maintaining peace in the region while also developing a sense of national identity apart from Russia's. Still, close ties to Russia remain. Russia is Kazakhstan's main trading partner and ally. Kazakhstan must also rely on Russia to handle imports and exports, since it is landlocked.

Kazakhstan's relationship with China has been a careful and strategic one. The Chinese are next-door neighbors, sharing several rivers necessary for trade for each country, as well as roads and rail links. Kazakhstan is a nation rich in oil, natural gas, and minerals, and China imports many of these resources. Kazakhstan also imports many of its goods from China—16 percent of its total imported goods in 2017. There are many Kazakhs living across the border in China, and since independence, many Chinese have bought property in Kazakhstan and are living there.

The United States was the first country to recognize Kazakhstan as an independent nation in 1991, opening an embassy in former capital Almaty in 1992. The United States imports oil and gas from Kazakhstan, in addition to iron, steel, chemicals, and uranium. Kazakhstan imports American machinery, aircraft, and many agricultural goods. Because of trade, the two countries maintain a good relationship.

Recent opportunities for change in Kazakhstan have opened doors to new ideas and dreams. However, with a new president just taking office and the old one still in the shadows, it will take some time to see what Kazakhstan's future will hold.

INTERNET LINKS

https://www.akorda.kz/en
This is the official website of the president of Kazakhstan. It gives details about the country, including national symbols, and about its leader.

http://www.government.kz/public/en
This is the official site for the government of Kazakhstan, including some of the latest government news.

http://mfa.gov.kz/en/hague/content-view/the-constitution-of-the -republic-of-kazakhstan
Explore the most recent constitution for the Republic of Kazakhstan.

ECONOMY

Workers check equipment flow valves at an oil field near the town of Akkystau in Kazakhstan.

KAZAKHSTAN HAS THE TOP economy among Central Asian countries. The backbone of this great economy is mining, since Kazakhstan is rich in fossil fuels, minerals, and metals like iron, manganese, nickel, copper, lead, and others. There is also a booming agricultural industry, producing grains like wheat and barley, potatoes, melons, and various livestock.

For most of Kazakhstan's modern history, its economy was closely tied to that of the Soviet Union. Its mineral resources were tapped and sent north to meet the production needs of Russian industry, which was developed to fulfill the demands of the Soviet consumer. Independence meant that Kazakhstan had to completely take charge of its economy and revamp its entire economic infrastructure. It is trying to reduce its dependence on the export of its natural resources by balancing this with a developing manufacturing industry. Russia remains a big part of Kazakhstan's economy but is becoming less so as Kazakhstan works to gain economic independence.

FOSSIL FUEL RESERVES

Of all its natural resources, oil is at present the country's most productive and lucrative. The oil reserves, found mainly in the northern end of the Caspian Sea, have been estimated to be as much as 30 billion barrels,

4

"Kazakhstan is a wonderland where colossal, almost unbelievable transformations can really happen."
—Wade Shepard for *Forbes* magazine

according to sources in the industry. Most of this is in new reserves that have not yet been exploited or even discovered.

The country's main oil reserves lie in the western part. There are currently three major oil fields: Tengiz, Kashagan, and Karachaganak. Tengiz is an onshore field near the Caspian Sea and is in the top 10 oil and gas fields in the world, yielding over 500,000 barrels each day. Kashagan, the fifth-largest oil field in the world, holds three times the amount of oil as Tengiz, but it is also expensive to operate. The offshore oil field began production in 2013, but it was announced in 2014 that Kashagan would be shut down for two years as repairs were made to pipelines damaged by toxic and corrosive hydrogen sulfide. After some expensive updates to the pipelines, the field was reopened in 2016. The Karachaganak field is situated in northwest Kazakhstan, close to the Russian border. It's smaller than both Tengiz and Kashagan, but it's a significant oil field, with a reserve of an estimated 1.4 billion tons (1.3 billion metric tons) of oil.

One big problem for Kazakhstan in expanding the export of oil is that, to reach Western customers, it has to rely on pipeline access through Russia. In the mid-1990s, the only way to export oil was through a northbound pipeline linking Atyrau in northwestern Kazakhstan with Samara in Russia. In 2001, a pipeline connected Kazakh oil fields with the Russian Black Sea port of Novorossiysk. Kazakhstan exports oil directly to China via pipeline, but to transport oil to Europe and farther west, the only options are to go through Russia or Iran, also oil-producing countries.

Kazakhstan also has enormous reserves of natural gas. Both Tengiz and Karachaganak are also natural gas fields, accounting for 70 percent of natural gas production in Kazakhstan. Until 2016, Kazakhstan was still importing natural gas from surrounding countries because no pipeline existed to transport natural gas within the country. The completion of the Beineu-Bozoi-Shymkent pipeline, linking the gas fields of the Caspian Sea region with the population centers of southern Kazakhstan, changed that. Kazakhstan also relies on regional pipeline networks to export its natural gas abroad. The Central Asia—Center pipeline, which lies along the western edge of the country, moves gas into Russia, while the Turkmenistan—China pipeline links with the

Beineu-Bozoi-Shymkent pipeline and carries gas along Kazakhstan's southern border and into China.

The country is also a major coal producer, mining nearly 118 million tons (107 million metric tons) in 2018. Coal primarily comes from the Karganady and Pavlodar regions in central and northeastern Kazakhstan. Much of the coal is used to produce power and to produce steel. In the initial years after independence, the coal industry in Kazakhstan saw a decline, due in part to the dangerous nature of coal mining, which kills or injures many workers. However, coal production has expanded in recent years.

Iron ore, manganese, chromite, lead, zinc, copper, titanium, bauxite, silver, phosphates, and cobalt are also mined in Kazakhstan. Since independence, other foreign countries have shown interest in developing these resources with the Kazakh government. Kazakhstan's gold-mining sector also continues to progress. In 2018, new technologies were being developed and planned for implementation in this industry.

"Oil has been pumped from this remote plain since the early 1990s at a pace that would have depleted other fields by now. Yet it is still gushing, and there is much more to come."

–Stanley Reed for the *New York Times*, on Tengiz

OTHER INDUSTRIES

Before 1991, Kazakhstan had a large manufacturing and processing industry. Following independence, industrial production remained one of the most important sectors of the economy. Today, one-fourth of all foreign investment goes to the manufacturing industry. There is a machine-building industry specializing

In 2012, then president Nazarbayev made an announcement as part of his annual state of the union address to Kazakhstan's citizens. By 2050, Kazakhstan would be among the top 30 global economies in the world. The strategy, called Kazakhstan 2050, would reform companies owned and run by the government, improve infrastructure, and attract foreign investors, bringing new businesses and industries to Kazakhstan. This would reduce the country's dependence on the oil and gas industry, since fossil fuels are a finite resource. One big challenge that Kazakhstan has faced is moving away from the ideals of an economy once controlled by the Soviet Union and adopting a capitalist framework upon which to base financial decisions. Kazakhstan's GDP jumped 4 percent from 2016 to 2017 and continues to grow each year.

in manufacturing construction equipment, tractors, bulldozers, agricultural machines, and military defense equipment. Metallurgy, or the processing of metals, and the production of chemicals, petrochemicals, and construction materials are also important. Light industries include the canning of fruits and vegetables, milling, brewing, and wine-making. In 2018, the country embarked on new technologies, such as facilities for manufacturing rail wheels, transformers, and cement, none of which had been manufactured in Kazakhstan before.

FARMING AND LIVESTOCK

Agriculture is also one of the top industries in Kazakhstan. The main agricultural regions are the north-central and southern parts of the country. Growing grain, especially wheat, is the main activity in the north-central region, while cotton and rice are the main crops in the south. Kazakhstan also produces meat, wool, and milk. Much of the agricultural land is under the control of the government and is leased out to farmers. Efforts to encourage private land ownership have been met with skepticism, and a 2016 plan to allow foreign investors to lease Kazakh farmland for 25-year periods sparked protests around the country.

The climate and soil are most suited to the grazing of animals, thus the traditional Kazakh nomadic lifestyle, where people follow their herds of sheep, cattle, camels, and horses as they graze on the open steppes. Nomadic life was disrupted when Soviet policy in the 1950s and 1960s introduced widespread cultivation of the land, and many nomads were forced to settle down and farm. Their herds were taken by the Soviet government. Today, 1 percent of Kazakhs are nomadic.

A Kazakh farmer drives a tractor and equipment to a field near Nur-Sultan.

A BUSY WORKFORCE

In the past, most workers were employed in state enterprises, and before independence, women made up about half of the total number of workers. This high participation of female workers meant that about 80 percent of the population of working age was employed. However, these high employment figures may not have been accurate because, until independence, it was Soviet policy not to acknowledge unemployment. Russians tended to have higher-paying, skilled jobs in sectors such as transportation, industry, and science, while Kazakhs predominated in the lower-paid jobs.

Since independence, large numbers of skilled managers and technicians, mainly of Russian or Slavic descent, have moved out of the country, and for some time, this affected the growth of the economy. However, other Kazakhs quickly filled in the gaps.

Today, the country's workforce is estimated to be about 9 million strong. There has been a push by the government to see that Kazakhs are well educated and able to participate in a higher level of services and industry and new technologies.

THE BANKING SYSTEM

Since 1993, the Kazakh banking system has been organized into two levels. At the top is the National Bank of Kazakhstan, which regulates the country's banking system and ensures that the national currency, the tenge, is strong and stable. All other commercial banks, whether private or owned by the state, comprise the second level.

The tenge was introduced in 1993 to replace the Soviet ruble as Kazakhstan's official currency. The first bills were printed in the United Kingdom (UK), while coins were minted in Germany. One US dollar equals about 380 tenge. The word tenge *in Kazakh means a set of scales, bringing in the idea of balance and equality. November 15, the day that the new national currency was introduced, is celebrated as the Day of National Currency of the Republic of Kazakhstan. The tenge was once the only currency in the world with two different languages on it: Kazakh and Russian. However, in 2019, the government announced that the nation's currency would go through a redesign, removing any language but Kazakh.*

The period immediately following independence was a time of great stress for the economy. Government price controls were removed, the rate of inflation rose, and the price of food, services, and other products got so high that the people's buying power was greatly reduced. There was a banking boom, and more than 200 small banks opened for business. However, the National Bank took control of the situation, strengthening banking laws and stabilizing the monetary system. In 2001, there were fewer than 50 banks operating. Foreign banks were prohibited for a long time from opening branches in Kazakhstan, but by 2019 this had changed, with 20 banks setting up offices in the country. The operation of these banks is still controlled by the National Bank.

IMPORTS AND EXPORTS

Before independence, Kazakhstan traded mainly with the Russian Federation. Today, Russia and China are Kazakhstan's biggest import and export partners, but the government is working hard to open the country up to more international trade by stabilizing the economy, deregulating, and liberalizing trade regulations. Kazakhstan's other top trade partners are France, the Netherlands, and Italy for exports, and Germany and the United States for imports.

In 2010, Kazakhstan joined with Russia and Belarus to form a customs union. The goal was to increase trade and foreign investment to these countries. In 2012, this became known as the Single Economic Space, and it became known as the Eurasian Economic Union (EAEU) in 2015, ultimately expanding to include Kyrgyzstan and Armenia. As of 2017, exports to other EAEU nations had increased by over 30 percent. Imports from the countries grew by over 24 percent.

Outside the EAEU, the country's increasingly stable government and abundant natural resources have attracted foreign investors to Kazakhstan. Among them are companies from Great Britain, the United States, and France. In 2018, the country established the Astana International Financial Centre (AIFC) with the hope of encouraging even more financial investment from overseas.

Likewise, there is a growing middle class of citizens who are eager to join foreign companies in taking advantage of the opportunities created by the increasing economic openness of the country. Foreign investment is important in the development of key sectors of Kazakh industry, especially the oil and gas, mining, and construction sectors. It will be interesting to see how the AIFC accomplishes its goals in the future.

IMPROVING INFRASTRUCTURE

Independent Kazakhstan inherited the poor telecommunications and transportation networks from its Soviet days. This was due to the generally inhospitable land that lay between populated areas. However, the country has been working hard to improve systems for its people. Today, Kazakhstan has one of the most advanced communications systems in Central Asia. A vast majority of people have access to 4G mobile networks and the internet. Mobile usage is very popular, as are broadband systems. Geolocation, online banking, and other technologies were in development as of 2018. As of 2019, Kazakhstan's five main cities hoped to have 5G capabilities within the next five years, while 2,616 settlements in rural areas were expected to receive broadband internet by 2020.

In terms of transportation, many cities are linked by both road and rail. Most freight is carried by rail or air. Almaty and Nur-Sultan have the two

THE RUSSIAN LAUNCH COMPLEX

Sending satellites into space is one of the more unusual ways Kazakhstan earns foreign exchange. The Baykonur Cosmodrome space facility was set up by the Soviets near the Kazakh town of Leninsk, though they named it after the faraway town of Baykonur to mislead Americans about the facility's location. Today, the town of Leninsk has itself come to be known as Baykonur. The facility can put a satellite into orbit for any country at a lower cost than that charged by the US National Aeronautics and Space Administration (NASA). Since NASA's shuttle program was retired in 2011, many US missions have launched from Kazakhstan's launch site. Baykunor Cosmodrome has been in operation since 1957, back when it was the base for Soviet launches. It was the launch site of Sputnik 1, *the first human-made satellite sent into space, and of* Vostok 1, *aboard which Yuri Gagarin became the first human in space. The complex is a bewildering network of launch pads, gantries, and tracking stations. Launches literally shake the earth. The Cosmodrome is co-funded and co-managed by both Russia and Kazakhstan. Russia continues to pay around $115 million to lease the land where the launch site sits.*

Shown here is Kazakhstan's largest international airport, in Almaty.

biggest and busiest airports, with connecting flights to Russia, member countries of the CIS, and China.

After independence, Kazakhstan Airlines was set up with 100 aircraft, part of the USSR's fleet that was divided among the former Soviet republics. It has since stopped operating. The country's national airline is now Air Astana, formed in 2001 by the government and a British aerospace company. Several private airline companies also operate in Kazakhstan, including the airlines of Ukraine and Uzbekistan; Lufthansa of Germany; British Airways; and Turkish, Iranian, and Russian airlines.

Kazakhstan has good road and rail links with Russia, China, and other Central Asian states. The Kazakhstan Temir Zholy (KTZ) company is the main railway organization for the country. Established in 2002, its high-speed lines link Kazakhstan with Russia and many other Asian countries. The Urumqi-Almaty line was completed in 1990, linking Kazakhstan with Xinjiang in China via a border crossing at Dostyk, also known as Druzhba, the Russian word for "friendship." In 2013, China launched the Belt and Road Initiative, investing in infrastructure that would ease transport of goods to Europe across Afghanistan, Kazakhstan, Uzbekistan, and other Asian countries. A major feature of the project was the creation of a "dry" port in Khorgos, on the Kazakh-Chinese border, where Chinese goods could be reloaded onto Kazakh trains for making the journey to Europe. Dubbed the Khorgos Gateway, the facility began operating in 2015.

Although Kazakhstan is landlocked, it has two inland river waterways—the Syr Darya River in the south-central region and the Irtysh (Ertis) River in the north. They are used to transport freight and passengers.

TECHNOLOGICAL IMPROVEMENTS

Advances in telecommunications have led to improvements in other sectors as well, including municipal and medical. Digitizing government services has also been in the works, bringing new technology to monitoring and managing traffic, shortening response time during an emergency, improving education across the country, and allowing hospitals to store all patient data online.

INTERNET LINKS

https://aifc.kz
This website explores the Astana International Financial Centre and contains up-to-date news about the AIFC's progress.

https://astanatimes.com/2018/12/kazakhstan-exports-to-110 -countries-continues-developing-manufacturing-industry
This article dives in to Kazakhstan's lead export and import partnerships.

https://www.worldbank.org/en/country/kazakhstan/overview
The World Bank website gives a brief overview of Kazakhstan's economy in the 21st century.

ENVIRONMENT

Issyk Lake, near Almaty, offers expansive, beautiful views of mountains, sky, and water.

KAZAKHSTAN'S ENVIRONMENT HAS faced problems in the 20th and 21st centuries. Many of the environmental issues that are a concern in Kazakhstan stem from Soviet industrialization and exploitation in the latter part of the 20th century. The results of nuclear testing before 1990 are still problematic for both environmental and human health in Kazakhstan. Industry has contaminated air and water, and excessive irrigation practices have shrunk the Aral Sea to half its former size. While Kazakhstan's government is working to improve conditions, there is no simple fix.

Kazakhstan remains a beautiful land, uniquely situated in the center of the Asian continent. The climate is difficult, and the land is fragile. It has hundreds of species of flora and fauna, many not found anywhere else in the world.

5

The Aral Sea, which exists in Kazakhstan and Uzbekistan, was once the world's fourth-largest freshwater lake. Today, it is one-tenth of its former size.

NUCLEAR TESTING AT SEMIPALATINSK

Since the 1950s, there has been an increase in Kazakh children born with physical and neurological abnormalities due to nuclear testing fallout. Many of these children end up in orphanages.

After World War II, the Soviet Union and the United States entered a rivalry called the Cold War. This non-fighting "war" involved the accumulation and stockpiling of nuclear weapons. As such, the Soviet Union needed to test its nuclear armament. It chose to do so in the wilds of Kazakhstan.

The Soviet Union's primary nuclear testing site from 1949 to 1989 was Semipalatinsk, also known as "the Polygon," a vast area of land near the city of Semey. Today, the area is overgrown with grass and totally abandoned. Radiation levels are still elevated, decades after the testing stopped. For generations of Kazakhs living within range of the former testing site, high levels of radiation have led to numerous health problems—primarily cancers. The memory of Semipalatinsk also runs deep.

The first nuclear test at Semipalatinsk, called First Lightning, was conducted in 1949. It scattered radioactive fallout on nearby villages, some of which were not evacuated. During Semipalatinsk's period of operation, more than 450 nuclear experiments were carried out. The cumulative impact of these experiments has been likened to several thousand times the impact of the atomic bomb that fell on Hiroshima, Japan, during World War II. Between 1949 and 1962, over 100 atmospheric (above-ground) nuclear weapons tests took place. This caused tremendous environmental pollution in the areas affected by the fallout and injured thousands of people over at least three generations who were exposed to the radiation. There were numerous birth defects and mutations and high incidences of cancer, immunological deficiencies, and other diseases among the population in the area that lasted for decades. Eventually, after 1962, Soviet scientists moved testing belowground. However, damage continued to linger. In 1996, after Kazakhstan had become its own country, cleanup of the area started. Crews from Kazakhstan, Russia, and America were sent on a mission to secure the area from highly radioactive materials that had been stored in underground tunnels and left. That endeavor lasted 17 years, costing $150 million.

The cleanup of Semipalatinsk after it was closed was spearheaded by the newly independent Kazakhstan, Russia, and an unlikely ally, the United States. American scientists who visited the site in 1995 believed that Semipalatinsk was vulnerable to terrorists and thieves looking for plutonium. Scientists believed that up to 450 pounds (204 kilograms) of nuclear material was left buried on the site, enough to build several nuclear bombs. Evidence that scavengers were digging at the site was already apparent. Borrowing an idea from the Chernobyl nuclear power plant disaster cleanup in Ukraine, the countries decided to build a concrete containment dome over one of the Semipalatinsk test areas, an effort called Operation Groundhog. The United States funded the project, which was completed in 2003. In 2004, similar measures were taken at another part of Semipalatinsk, the Degelen Mountain bunker, which contained about 220 pounds (100 kg) of plutonium. In 2012, the entire area was deemed secure.

A POLLUTION PROBLEM

Today, land use in Kazakhstan continues to be traditional. Over 75 percent of the land is under agricultural use—much of it for pasturing animals. The environmental problems facing Kazakhstan are natural as well as man-made. People living in the river valleys and fertile areas around the rivers have a tremendous impact on the country's fragile water ecosystems. Agriculture puts a strain on water resources through overuse of water, need for irrigation, and pollution.

A Kazakh muralist in the 1990s used this piece to protest oil pollution. The artist's home city of Atyrau is a fishing center that was affected by pollution.

Urbanization and industrialization have created additional problems of pollution. The mining industry has indiscriminately dumped materials such as tailings, ash, rubble, and other waste products on the land. Kazakhstan is fortunate to have enormous reserves of oil, but the extraction of these resources has also been environmentally detrimental, transforming large areas of natural or agricultural land. Oil production requires a tremendous infrastructure—thousands of miles of pipeline, roads, oil wells, and support buildings have to be constructed. This results in loss of habitat for plants and animals growing where advancements are being made.

Extracting oil is an environmentally risky business. The risks are not unique to Kazakhstan, however. Wherever oil is being taken from the ground, it disrupts the natural environment, be it fragile steppe land, rain forest, or an ocean habitat. Environmentalists are seeing the effects of oil-related pollution in the Caspian Sea as seal, turtle, and fish populations decrease.

Air pollution, particularly in the cities and industrial centers, is high. The main polluting industries are ferrous and nonferrous metallurgy, the production of heat and energy, chemical and oil processing, and mineral fertilizer production. Plants in industrial areas emit pollutants and effluent with very little control. Many cities, such as Almaty, Shymkent, Taraz, Ekibastuz, and Pavlodar, have many times the maximum admissible concentration of pollutants such as sulfur dioxide, zinc, chrome, lead, iron, chlorine, and mercury, just to name a few. The increasing number of automobiles releasing gases into the atmosphere is adding to the problem. As a result, many people become ill or die from respiratory diseases.

OTHER ENVIRONMENTAL CONCERNS

Agriculture, industry, and urbanization are the main sources of environmental concern in most countries. In Kazakhstan, however, there is an additional, unique environmental concern resulting from nuclear testing and rocket launching. The sites associated with former defense industries and test ranges are radioactive and chemically toxic. They pose a severe health risk to people and animals.

All these problems are compounded by the fact that Kazakhstan also has a very fragile natural environment. According to the Kazakh government, large areas of southern Kazakhstan are vulnerable to wind erosion. Soil erosion due to water runoff is also a problem. Much of the country's water supply has been polluted by industrial and agricultural runoff. Other aspects affecting the environment today are climate change and desertification, or the spreading of deserts across a land. As of 2019, Kazakhstan had become victim to several marks of climate change, including more frequent droughts and flooding. Organizations such as the World Health Organization (WHO) predict these incidents will further intensify in the future. As a precaution, Kazakhstan joined the Kyoto Protocol of 1997 and the Paris Climate Agreement of 2016, agreeing to contribute to the worldwide effort to lower carbon emissions.

Chemical contamination of the water has killed and made life difficult for the flora and fauna that depend upon water ecosystems in this nation, from the smallest living organisms such as bacteria and algae to larger fish, plants, and animals. The two main rivers that flowed into the Aral Sea have been diverted for irrigation. As a result, the sea is drying up and leaving behind a layer of chemical pesticides and natural salts. These substances are then picked up by the wind.

These wild ducks at High Tainty Lake in Kazakhstan are just one species affected by water pollution.

SAVING THE ARAL SEA

Kazakhstan shares the Aral Sea with neighboring Uzbekistan. In ancient times, this sea was a fertile and rich area, providing a livelihood for the traders, hunters, and fishing people who lived here. The word *aral* in Kazakh means "island." This was a reference to the more than 1,000 islands that dotted these waters.

The Aral Sea was once an important stopping point along the Silk Road linking Europe and Asia. Once it was the fourth-largest lake in the world. Today, the sea is very much reduced in size. It has shrunk so much that it is now composed of three smaller, separate bodies of water—the North Aral Sea in Kazakhstan and the mostly Uzbek eastern and western basins of the South Aral Sea. This is because the two rivers that feed into the Aral Sea, the Amu Darya and the Syr Darya, have been diverted for irrigating agricultural lands. It was part of the Soviet plan to regenerate the surrounding desert for the growing of crops.

As the lake dried up, it increased in salinity to such an extent that it became toxic for the fish and wildlife that used to depend upon it. Many people who

used to fish there, especially in Uzbekistan, have abandoned their livelihood. One can still see abandoned fishing boats and other equipment littering the dry and dusty Aral shores. The winds that blow across the land pick up the salt and dust and carry it miles away. The dust carries an unhealthy amount of chemicals from pesticides and fertilizers.

This creates a health problem for the people in the region, including an increase in cancers and cardiovascular, tubercular, and respiratory diseases. Kazakhstan; its neighbors Uzbekistan, Tajikistan, Turkmenistan, and Kyrgyzstan; and international organizations are trying to reverse the Aral Sea tragedy, which has been described as one of the world's worst environmental disasters.

In the 21st century, Kazakhstan has worked to revive the sea. In 2014, the World Bank stepped in with an $87 million project to construct a dam between the northern part of the sea and the southern part of the sea. The hope was the dam would keep more water in the North Aral Sea. Completed in 2005, it became known as the Kok-Aral Dam. Today, the efforts being put forth by scientists and others include the creation of more dams to help fill the sea, improving the quality of irrigation canals, moving away from water-intensive crops, and redirecting water from other rivers into the sea. By 2019, it seemed that their efforts were working in the north. While the Aral Sea remains only about one-tenth of its former size, the fishing industry in Kazakhstan seems to be bouncing back. In 1946, 25,000 tons (23,000 metric tons) of fish were caught by fishermen in the waters of the Aral Sea. By 1996, this number fell to only 33 tons (30 metric tons). By 2016, the annual catch topped 7,000 tons (6,350 metric tons). It is hoped that similar success can be directed toward the South Aral Sea in years to come, so communities once flourishing near the sea can resurge.

CARING FOR KAZAKHSTAN

The Ministry of Ecology, Geology, and Natural Resources, formerly the Ministry of Environment Protection, is the department of the Kazakh government that works with United Nations (UN) agencies, nongovernmental organizations, community groups, and individuals to redress environmental problems, manage water supplies, and see that protective legislation is in place. The ministry has identified a number of important and distinctively different ecological systems in Kazakhstan. These are the high-altitude mountain ecological system, the forest steppes, the grass steppes, the desert areas, and the wetlands.

There are four large mountainous regions mostly in the western part of the country—the Western Tien Shan, Northern Tien Shan, Kazakhstan-Dzhungar, and Altai ranges. Although these are relatively inaccessible areas because of altitude, nevertheless they have been much altered and disturbed by agriculture, forestry, recreational needs, and the construction of roads and cities.

The forest steppes are in the north, covering the region of the cities of Petropavl and Kokshetau. Although this is a small region overall, these steppes are an important ecological anchor because they are rich in various types of grass, and they protect the soils of the adjacent steppe lands.

WHAT KILLED THE SAIGA ANTELOPE?

In 2015, scientists were baffled when suddenly more than 200,000 saiga antelope died—around 60 percent of the world's total population— littering a region of central Kazakhstan with bodies. Three years later, researchers reported that the deaths were due to a bacterial infection. The bacteria is commonly present in this species of antelope, but factors such as heightened heat

and humidity, possibly due to climate change, might have turned a minor issue into a catastrophe. The saiga antelope is a protected species in Kazakhstan. Populations had dwindled greatly because of poachers but were beginning to bounce back when the mass die-off occurred. Scientists are hopeful that the population will bounce back again, however. Female saiga are capable of reproducing within the first year of their lives.

The Kazakhstan steppe is the ecological zone that has been most transformed by human activity. There was wide-scale plowing and opening up of the land to agriculture, especially during the Virgin Land period from 1954 to 1960. This destroyed much of the natural grasses, and in their place, weeds have been introduced into these areas that were made arable.

In the desert areas, the worst destruction of plant cover has occurred in the foothill zones, where the land was used for the pasturing of animals and trees were cut for fuel. This has caused soil erosion and increasing desertification, making areas that were once agriculturally productive into infertile land.

PROTECTING THE ENVIRONMENT

Kazakhstan's wet and marshy areas lie in the north. Here, thousands of lakes are important nesting areas for local sandpipers, seagulls, terns, and other waterfowl. Being situated in the center of the Asian continent, this area is also a crucial nesting and resting site for many bird species migrating from Siberia to the Caspian Sea and between Asia and Africa. Some of the most popular nesting sites include Korgalzhyn State Nature Reserve and Naurzum Nature Reserve.

The government is aware that it has to balance the need to develop the land and use its resources for the country's economic growth with the necessity of preserving the unique heritage of Kazakhstan's natural wealth. It has established many national parks and nature and game reserves. These reserves preserve special ecosystems such as the mountains, desert, lakes, forests, and the vast steppes. These areas are under the protection of the Ministry of Ecology, Geology, and Natural Resources.

Kazakhstan has signed a number of international environmental agreements, such as the UN Convention on Biological Diversity of 1992, the Kyoto Protocol, and the Paris Climate Agreement. In a number of areas, it has to work with its neighbors to protect natural resources that these various countries share. For instance, Kazakhstan, Uzbekistan, and Kyrgyzstan are committed to the conservation of the Western Tien Shan region, which is listed by the United Nations Educational, Scientific, and Cultural Organization (UNESCO) as a World Heritage site for its rich biodiversity.

The Aksu-Zhabagly Nature Reserve in southern Kazakhstan, set up in 1927 at the foot of the Tien Shan Mountains, is the oldest established nature reserve in Kazakhstan and probably all of Central Asia. It covers more than 210,000 acres (85,000 hectares). Here can be found thousands of plant species, more than 200 bird species, and almost 50 different species of animals. It is home to the Siberian ibex, roe and Caspian deer, boars, weasels, and vultures. Among the rare and endangered animals in this reserve are the snow leopard, the Turkestan lynx, the Pamir argali, the red bear, the golden eagle (Kazakhstan's national bird), the saker falcon, and the short-toed eagle. The Karabastau and Akbastau paleontological sites on the slopes of the Karatau Mountains have fossils of fish, mollusks, tortoises, and insects from the Jurassic period because this area was once under the sea.

The Naurzum Nature Reserve, covering more than 215,000 acres (87,000 ha) in the Kostanay region, is the second-oldest reserve in Kazakhstan. It was set up primarily to preserve the Naurzum pine forest. However, the wetlands of the reserve are also an important habitat for numerous bird species, many of

A golden eagle spreads its wings over Kazakhstan, with the Tien Shan Mountains in the background.

them endangered. The white heron is one of the rare and interesting inhabitants of the reserve.

In the 1960s and later, Kazakhstan established many more reserves, among them the Korgalzhyn, Almaty, Markakol, Ustyurt, and West-Altai Reserves. Korgalzhyn in the Akmola region is the sanctuary of the pink flamingo, whose nests in Lake Tengiz are the northernmost of its species in the world. In addition, the reserve attracts migratory waterfowl and other birds such as the Dalmatian pelican and mute swan. This swampy, marshy reserve has been designated a protected landscape by UNESCO. In 2018, the Ile-Balkhash State Reserve joined the list as the newest nature reserve in Kazakhstan. It spans over 1 million acres (415,000 ha) and was developed in part to decrease Kazakhstan's carbon footprint and commit to tackling environmental issues such as climate change.

In addition to nature reserves, a number of national parks have also been established. Altyn-Emel National Park in the Almaty region is especially known for a natural phenomenon called sand barchans. These crescent-shaped sand dunes are called "singing sands" for the loud sounds they produce when the wind blows over them or when one walks on them. A similar phenomenon can be found in California's Kelso Dunes and Eureka Dunes and the Warren Dunes of southwestern Michigan. Meanwhile, Sayram-Ugam National Park protects species of boar, wolves, and bobcats. Karkaraly National Park's unique rock formations are home to a number of eagles. Buyratau National Park is home to 200 bird species, 450 plant species, and wild sheep.

INTERNET LINKS

https://caravanistan.com/best-of/kazakhstan-nature-national -parks
The Caravanistan travel site offers a look at some of Kazakhstan's national parks and nature reserves.

https://www.nationalgeographic.com/photography/proof/2017/10/ nuclear-ghosts-kazakhstan
National Geographic shares some pictures and memories from those who were and continue to be affected by nuclear testing at Semipalatinsk.

https://www.worldatlas.com/articles/endangered-mammals-of -kazakhstan.html
Readers can learn more about some of the endangered species of Kazakhstan on the World Atlas website.

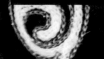

KAZAKHS

A Kazakh nomadic woman poses for a picture.

6

THE POPULATION OF KAZAKHSTAN was estimated at over 18.5 million as of 2019, and more Kazakhs are arriving each year, returning to a homeland they were once forced to abandon. During Soviet rule of Kazakhstan, Kazakhs were expected to eschew their traditional nomadic lifestyle in favor of settling in one place and farming. Their herds were confiscated. Much of the land was settled by Russian and Ukrainian farmers. This system resulted in famine, and over a million Kazakhs died as a result. Others fled to surrounding countries and were treated as traitors by the Soviet government. After the collapse of the Soviet Union, many Russians have returned to Russia, and Kazakhs have slowly begun to return to their homeland.

The Kazakhs emerged as a separate and recognizable group sometime in the middle of the 15th century. Their ancestors were nomadic people

Traditionally, Kazakh men wear a chapan, a wraparound robe made of cotton or wool and fastened with a belt at the waist. It looks like a dressing gown. The women wear colorful, sleeveless velvet jackets that are often ornately embroidered. The men wear caps on their heads, and the women wear head scarves. Today, it is more common to see Kazakhs in modern dress, while traditional clothing is less common.

Fashion has become increasingly important in Kazakhstan in the decades following independence. Kazakhstan's first Fashion Week was held in 1999 and has become an annual occurrence. Much of Kazakhstan's fashion combines modern style with traditional Kazakh dress.

Traditional styles of dress are still worn in Kazakhstan for special occasions and ceremonies.

from a mixture of Turkic tribes who had lived in the area for centuries. Turkic people are descended from the Turks who, according to historians, were the first people to speak a Turkic language. A very powerful Turk Empire ruled Central Asia beginning in the sixth century CE. Although it was a short-lived empire, the Turks left behind a long-lasting legacy and left their mark on all the people of Central Asia.

After the Turks came a long line of different empires. There were the Uighurs, the Kyrgyz, the Khitans, the Mongols, and the Uzbeks. Both the modern Uzbeks and Kazakhs were formed from a blurred ancestry of the overlapping tribes and peoples of Central Asia.

HORDES OF KAZAKHSTAN

Historically, Kazakhs can be divided into three clans, or hordes. Each clan had its own territory. Kazakhs of the Lesser Horde came from western Kazakhstan, between the Aral Sea and the Ural River; the Middle Horde dominated the northern and central part of Kazakhstan east of the Aral Sea; and the Great Horde belonged to the southeastern area north of the Tien Shan Mountains.

Kazakhs of the Lesser and Middle Hordes were the first to come under Russian domination and tend to be more Russified, or more observant of Russian traditions and practices. Many of their children were sent to study in Russian schools. Early Kazakh nationalists were often from these Lesser and Middle Hordes. They involved themselves in politics even before the Russian Revolution and were the targets of Stalin's purges during the 1930s, when he tried to get rid of the Kazakh intelligentsia.

The architecture of this wooden house in Kazakhstan is a popular Russian style.

The Great Horde Kazakhs were the last to come under Russian control because, being in the south, they were farthest away from Russia. They were politicized only after the revolution, but members of the Great Horde have dominated Kazakh politics. This was especially evident when the capital of the country was moved to Almaty in the south. Soviet Kazakh leader Dinmukhamed Kunayev belonged to the Great Horde, and so does former president Nursultan Nazarbayev.

Most Russians in Kazakhstan live in the north, where they are close to Russia. Moving the capital from Almaty in the south to Nur-Sultan in the north-central region was partly designed to make the area more Kazakh-dominated. About three-fifths of ethnic Kazakhs live in the countryside. Kazakh cities have grown more as a result of migration into the nation than as a result of the movement of Kazakhs from the countryside to the cities. Nevertheless, over half of the country's population lives in urban areas. As of 2019, Almaty boasted a population of almost 1.9 million people, Nur-Sultan was home to 1.1 million, and Shymkent had a population of just over 1 million.

RUSSIANS AND SLAVS

Russians make up the largest minority group in Kazakhstan. Most of them live in the cities of the steppes and plains in the north. Living in northern Kazakhstan means that Russia is just a day's drive away. The rest of the population is made up mostly of the other major ethnic groups of Central Asia—Uzbeks, Ukrainians, and Uighurs.

Between the 1860s and 1930s, 180,000 Koreans settled in Russia to escape Japanese oppression. However, in 1937, Koreans living in Russia were deported, many to Kazakhstan, by Stalin, who believed that Koreans might be spies for the Japanese, with whom the Soviet Union was in conflict. Those who survived the grueling winter journey by train—40,000 didn't—were expected to grow rice, a difficult task in the dry steppes of Kazakhstan. They were promised supplies and money, but the materials never arrived. They were banned from learning their own language, and their books were destroyed. However, the Koryo Saram (meaning "people of Korea") maintained a sense of identity and culture. Many Koryo Saram still live in Kazakhstan today.

People dressed in traditional Kazakh costumes celebrate an end-of- winter festival in Shymkent in 2018.

The Russians began their invasion of Central Asia in the late 16th century, establishing small forts along the way and completing their advance eastward to the Pacific Ocean by the middle of the 17th century. Russian traders and soldiers arrived on the northeast edge of the Kazakh territory in the 17th century, when Cossacks established the forts that later became the cities of Uralsk and Atyrau. The Russian takeover was made easier when the Kazakhs, pressured by the threat of invasions from China in the east, allied themselves with the Russian Empire.

The Russian soldiers were followed by Russian settlers. They cultivated the land and formed settlements around the forts. During the 19th century, there was a flood of immigrants to the region. About 400,000 Russians arrived, followed by about 1 million others, including Slavs, Germans, and Jews, who arrived during the first part of the 20th century.

Another large influx of Russians and Slavs occurred in the 1950s during the Virgin and Idle Lands project that was initiated by Nikita Khrushchev. These people settled in the rich agricultural areas in the north. Today, many Russians are beginning to return to their home country. President Nazarbayev's departure from office further prompted the exodus. Experts believe that in

RETURN TO KAZAKHSTAN

Oralmans is a name given to over a million Kazakhs returning to their home country, sometimes generations later, now that Kazakhstan is an independent nation. These returnees are coming from surrounding countries like Uzbekistan, China, Mongolia, Turkmenistan, Russia, and others. The process hasn't been easy, though. To return to Kazakhstan, ethnic Kazakhs must abandon their current country's citizenship. Communist-run China, in particular, hasn't made leaving easy or safe. Many Kazakhs have been detained and held in camps in China intended to "reeducate" Muslims, many of them Kazakh. These detainees have reported extreme acts of violence at the camps. Once Kazakhs make it to Kazakhstan, many struggle to find and keep work or even to provide the documentation required for Kazakh citizenship. Oralmans are often blamed when there's unrest or violence in Kazakhstan. The term "oralman" itself has become a slur, and many prefer the terms "repatriate" or "kandas," which means "of common blood."

a few decades the number of Russians living in Kazakhstan will drop to only around 10 percent of the population. Currently, it hovers around 19 percent.

Once one of the largest cultural groups in Kazakhstan, today the Slavs are concentrated mainly in the country's cities. They work a variety of jobs. However, more recently, they have been emigrating to other countries, seeking new opportunities and making room for more ethnic Kazakhs to reside in their stead.

A POPULATION OF UNDESIRABLES

Between 1935 and 1940, Russia deported about 120,000 Poles from other areas of the Soviet Union to Kazakhstan. During World War II, Soviet leader Joseph Stalin used Kazakhstan as a dumping ground for many groups of people that the Soviets regarded as "problems." The Germans who lived in the Volga region of the Soviet Union were deported because it was feared that they might help the enemy, Nazi Germany. Germans had actually lived in the Volga region for almost two centuries, but their loyalty to the

Soviet Union was nevertheless called into question. They were sent to Kazakhstan and Siberia with little food to sustain them.

The Crimean Tatars were another group of people targeted during the war. The Tatars were people who were descended from the Mongols and had settled in the Crimean region. Stalin was afraid that they, too, might help the invading German army because they had suffered under the Soviet policy of collectivization. However, Nazi Germany invaded the region before the Tatars could be deported. When the Soviet Union won the war and recaptured the Crimean region, the Tatars were deported to Uzbekistan and Kazakhstan as punishment. Their villages were destroyed, and all evidence of their culture was erased. The Tatars claim that as many as 110,000 of their people died by 1946.

After independence, many non-Kazakhs left Kazakhstan, going to other former Soviet republics. Many of them were technicians and skilled workers. At the same time, the government encouraged Kazakhs from other parts of

This 2014 candlelight vigil in Kiev, Ukraine, honors the Crimean Tatars who were deported to Kazakhstan in the 1940s.

CENTRAL ASIA AND KAZAKHSTAN

It is helpful to see the Kazakhs in the larger context of Central Asia. They are ethnically and linguistically linked with the other major groups in the region. The Kazakhs are the largest ethnic group in Kazakhstan. Other large ethnic groups are the Uzbeks, Uighurs, and Tajiks. They share a common religion, Islam, which was brought to the southern parts of Central Asia in the seventh century and later spread north. Except for the Persian Tajiks, Kazakhs and other Central Asians belong to the larger Turkic ethnic group. Again, except for the Tajiks, they speak languages from the Turkic language family. The Tajiks speak an Indo-European language, part of a group of languages spoken for centuries across regions in Europe and southern Asia.

Today, around 47,000 Tajiks call Kazakhstan home. They have been working hard for years to promote their language and culture to the wider community. In 2009, a Tajik cultural center was created. Today, it hosts a variety of cultural celebrations, such as art festivals, music festivals, and language classes.

the former Soviet Union and China to return to their country. As a result of an uncertain future in Mongolia, Kazakhs living there also returned. Returning Kazakhs were promised housing, plots of land, and tax exemptions for two years, although many continue to struggle even decades later.

INTERNET LINKS

https://astanatimes.com/2018/12/tajik-cultural-heritage-local -culture-awareness-encouraged-in-kazakhstan-says-community -leader
This article discusses the Tajik cultural center in Almaty and the desire of the community to share their culture with others in the country.

http://www.thestoryinstitute.com/the-koreans-of-kazakhstan
Readers can learn more about the Koryo Saram people of Kazakhstan at the Story Institute's website.

LIFESTYLE

Friends and family dressed in their finest gather for a pasture picnic near the mountain village of Saty.

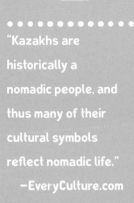

7

M UCH OF THE KAZAKH LIFESTYLE hearkens back to a time when people drew values from family and tradition. Although for most Kazakhs, the nomadic lifestyle is only part of their ancestry, the clan tradition of caring for and respecting one's elders is still a part of life in Kazakhstan. Many other traditions are also celebrated and continue to define life for most Kazakhs.

"Kazakhs are historically a nomadic people, and thus many of their cultural symbols reflect nomadic life."
—EveryCulture.com

A NOMADIC LIFE

Nomads once made up the majority of people in Kazakhstan's countryside. A nomad's life was essentially a difficult one. Each tribe had a hereditary route of migration and campsites that they used every year when they moved their herds from winter to summer grazing. No group was allowed to use the grazing lands of another.

Nomads lived at their main campsite during the winter. They normally spent four to five months a year there. The site was carefully chosen—it had to be sheltered and have ample water and grazing opportunities. Once they arrived at the campsite, they built their yurts, which were tent-like structures. In some cases, they instead created shelters from mounds of dirt, sticks, and stones.

The life of a traditional Kazakh nomad is not an easy one.

Winter was a period of rest. Being in one area for a few months allowed the nomads to make clothes and other items that they would need during the long trek back to their summer camp.

Once the snow melted and the new grass began to grow, the nomads would begin the spring migration to their summer campsites. Travel was slow, as they stopped every few days and set up camp wherever there was a source of water. They proceeded in this fashion until they reached their summer camp, usually by May or June.

On reaching the summer pastures, the group divided into smaller units and spread out so that their animals had a greater area for grazing. When they broke up into smaller units, "runners" carried messages between the groups. During the summer, the campsite might be moved several times within the general area if the grass or water became exhausted. The nomads remained at this campsite until August or September, when all groups reassembled for the long trek back to their winter site.

The distances that the nomads covered during their migration varied from region to region—anything from 125 to 185 miles (200 to 300 km) in the south to as much as 620 miles (1,000 km) in the western and central parts of the country.

Each Kazakh household had its own herd, but the animals grazed together with the herds of other households. Kazakhs owned both sheep and goats, which they valued very much because sheep and goats could provide them with food and clothing. They were also easy to feed as they ate all kinds of grass. But the animal that the Kazakhs truly treasured was the horse. It was the horse that made their nomadic lifestyle possible. They could ride their horses and use them to carry household possessions. The central and southern Kazakhs often used camels instead of horses. Cattle were more commonly used in the north.

The nomads' biggest problem was the weather. If the winter was harsh, their animals would starve, especially if storms covered the grass with ice that was impenetrable. Kazakhs called this phenomenon a *zhut* (JART) and still do today. Zhuts occur about once every 10 to 12 years. In the summer, drought was a problem for nomads. They dug shallow wells along their migration routes, and these could dry up in years when there was little rain. The salinity of the lakes and rivers on the steppes was an additional problem. As a result of this harsh and demanding life, people had to depend on each other for survival, so family relationships became very important.

In modern Kazakhstan, the true nomadic life has mostly disappeared, but some Kazakhs do engage in a seminomadic life, moving their herds and flocks to summer pastures every year. Tourist attractions also resurrect the nomadic life, offering visitors overnight stays in yurts or camel rides through the landscape.

The dome-shaped yurt dwelling has been the chosen home of nomadic Kazakhs because it can be easily moved from place to place.

A TRADITIONAL DWELLING

The traditional Kazakh dwelling is the yurt. This is a dome-shaped, tent-like structure made of a flexible framework of willow wood that is covered with layers of felt for warmth. An opening at the top that can be opened and shut allows smoke from the central stove to escape and allows occupants of the yurt to control the temperature. A yurt weighs about 550 pounds (250 kg) in all. It takes about an hour and a half to put it up.

The floor is the first part to be assembled, then the walls, which are made up of several sections of wooden latticework. The lattice is made of thin, wooden strips that are crisscrossed and can be opened and shut like an accordion. These sections are tied together to make a circle. There may be as many as 12 sections needed to make up the walls of a large yurt. After these are fit together with the door, the next step is to put up wooden posts in the middle, which will hold the roof up.

A small wooden wheel for the center of the roof is balanced on top of the posts. Then, wooden spokes are radiated from the wheel to the walls. Everything is carefully tied together. Over this skeleton structure is attached

This Kazakh bride wears a traditional dress for a photo, although many brides have switched to Western styles of dress.

a layer of canvas and blankets of felt. In the winter, thicker layers of felt are used. Another layer of canvas is thrown over the felt to keep out the rain. There is a small opening left at the very center so that air can circulate in the yurt and smoke from the cooking can escape.

Although the yurt is really one big open space, there are areas that are designated for special functions. The sleeping quarters are toward the back of the yurt, while cooking is done on the stove in the center. Visitors are entertained near the front. The right side is usually reserved for the men and the left for the women.

LOVE AND MARRIAGE

In the past, girls married at age 13 or 14, and men when they were one or two years older. Today, however, the bride and groom have to be 18 years of age, and both have to agree to the marriage. Different marriage customs exist in the country, including more Western weddings, but ancient rituals are also coming back into fashion. Traditionally, the engagement ceremony involves the groom's parents visiting the bride's parents to discuss a payment (called a *kalyn*) for the bride and her dowry. The dowry includes new clothes for the bride, a carpet, bed linen, and other household items, and a big trunk to hold these items. The payment depends on the wealth of the groom's family and is often paid in livestock. It can range from a few hundred sheep, camels, horses, and cows to several thousand cattle. If the bride's family agrees to the amount, the groom's father gives her father earrings and owl's feathers. Five or six relatives of the groom then visit the bride's father for a meal. The father gives each of them an animal as a sign of goodwill. The groom and his parents also give presents to the bride's parents and relatives on the wedding day. Sometimes, thousands of guests are invited to the wedding.

FAMILY INHERITANCE

Each of the three hordes is subdivided into patrilineal lines—that is, inheritance, descent, and kinship follows the male line. When a man dies, he passes on the

Age is a positive attribute and one that is associated with wisdom. Kazakhs show great respect for their elders. This is one of the binding elements of Kazakh society and is known as the "way of the elders." Elders are treated with honor and deference whenever they are present, whether at home or elsewhere. Elders are always consulted to give advice, to solve problems, and to make decisions that everyone respects and obeys. In the past, it was imperative to obey an elder, and anyone who did not do so was punished. In this way, the social structure was maintained. The same kind of deferential attitude shown to an elder is also shown to someone seen to be in a higher social position, such as a doctor or a teacher. A student would never criticize a teacher, nor would a junior worker criticize a supervisor.

family responsibilities to his eldest son, and his herds are divided among all his sons.

Historically, women did not have a share of the inheritance. The exceptions were an unmarried daughter, who received part of the livestock, and a widow, who took charge of the livestock if her sons were still too young. Although women did not have inheritance rights, they were strong members of society and were consulted on all matters of importance.

In modern Kazakhstan, women have gained equality with men, and their family and inheritance rights are fully protected by law.

Kazakh families spend lots of time together.

THE FAMILY NETWORK

As a result of the ties of marriage and kinship, a Kazakh man enjoys the support of his relatives. He knows he can draw on the resources and the network of his relatives in times of need. He has three networks of relatives—his father's relatives, his mother's relatives, and his wife's relatives.

It is not unusual for a Kazakh living in the city to have his distant cousin suddenly arrive from the countryside for a visit. He is obliged to provide a meal and even a bed for his relative, who usually comes with gifts.

As more and more Kazakhs move to the country's urban centers, a divide continues to grow between Kazakhstan's traditional way of life and a drive toward modern ideas. Kazakhstan is working to leave its Soviet past behind. In Almaty and Nur-Sultan, architects are designing hotels, casinos, movie theaters, skyscrapers, and American-style restaurants, moving away from the utilitarian styles of Soviet buildings and homes. Because Kazakhstan has only been an independent nation for a short time, urban centers are still in development. Kazakhs hope that building up urban centers will help with economic growth. By 2050, the Kazakh government hopes that 70 percent of the country's population will reside in its urban areas.

Patients wait in line to be seen by a doctor at a hospital in Shymkent.

These obligations are extended to include a whole network of relationships, so a Kazakh may also call on the services and help of old friends, schoolmates, and fellow workers. The bigger and stronger a family's social connections are, the more favors can be requested. This is useful when a family member needs to get a job, obtain a permit, bypass some government regulation, obtain medical services, get a discount for a purchase, or send a child to college.

BASIC HEALTH CARE

In 1991, the newly independent Kazakhstan had a well-established public health system that provided free medical care not only in the cities but also in the remote regions. This was a legacy from the Soviet system. However, the difficult years that immediately followed independence affected this public health service. The main problem was a lack of funds.

In the early 2000s, the government committed to completely reforming the health-care system. Officials focused on more accessible health-care options and primary health-care facilities. Today, many primary health clinics are scattered throughout the country as a result.

Since 2005, the government has been working to modernize rural hospitals and build more outpatient clinics in urban centers. Medical professionals have been becoming more prevalent as well. As of 2014, there were 3.25 doctors for every 1,000 Kazakh citizens. Kazakhstan's most popular hospitals are based in larger cities, such as Almaty and Nur-Sultan. The challenge for the future is to use financial resources to provide better and more efficient health care.

BIRTH AND DEATH

The population of Kazakhstan is slowly increasing. In 2018, the birthrate was 17.5 births for every 1,000 of the total population. Meanwhile, the death rate stood at around 8.2 deaths per 1,000 people. Cardiovascular diseases, tuberculosis, diabetes, and cancer are some of the country's major health problems.

Since the 1990s, the declining birthrate has become a matter of state concern, and Kazakh nationalist parties have tried to ban birth control and abortions. Despite this effort, 54 percent of families use contraceptives today. Abortion is also available and subsidized by the government, although the numbers for that are decreasing because of increased availability of low-cost or free contraception methods.

LITERACY AND SCHOOLS

Education is mandatory and free through secondary school. Russian was the only official language before independence. After independence, however, Kazakh became the second official language. In the early 1990s, schools continued to teach in Russian because there was a shortage of Kazakh textbooks and teachers. Now that the government favors the Kazakh language and has begun to phase out Russian and the Cyrillic alphabet, more Russians are sending their children to Russia for their education. Local teachers are required to have a fluent knowledge of Kazakh, and this has led to more Kazakh teachers in primary and secondary schools.

Kazakhstan has a very high literacy rate of about 99.8 percent. Both boys and girls tend to remain in school until they are about 15 years old. Private education is allowed but is closely supervised and controlled by the state. More than 90 percent of children of primary and secondary school age attend school. After secondary education, students have many choices for postsecondary education, as there are many universities and colleges in the country. Of these, the largest is the Al-Farabi Kazakh National University in Almaty.

There was a reorganization of the school curriculum and changes in the textbooks after independence. Today, Kazakh history, culture, and literature are getting greater attention. This has an effect not only in regular schools but also in institutions of higher learning. The National Kazakhstan Academy of Sciences, a body of scientists and academics dedicated to scientific advancement, was

Kazakhstan has traditionally been a patriarchal society, deferring to the man in instances of work, household leadership, and civil service. However, in the early 2000s, the country began adopting policies that promoted full equality between men and women. In 2009, the Law on State Guarantees of Equal Rights and Opportunities for Men and Women was passed. This law governs the country's gender policy. Another law, the Concept of Family and Gender Policy, passed in 2016, works to ensure that all citizens have equal rights and that those rights are protected, including the right to be protected against gender-based discrimination. Other initiatives the country is involved in include the UN Convention on Eliminations of All Forms of Discrimination Against Women and the Convention on the Political Rights of Women. However, despite these moves forward, the country still faces gender inequality, and women are not always treated well. As an example, a recent survey showed that over 17 percent of women have been subjected to domestic violence at some time in their life.

once Soviet controlled, but today its contributors are free to focus on sciences of their choosing, as well as the humanities.

THE TRADITION OF FEASTING

Connected with kinship bonds is the practice of holding feasts. Feasts and the giving of gifts that accompanies them take up a large proportion of a Kazakh's time and money. It is not merely because celebrations are enjoyed and that everyone loves to receive gifts that Kazakhs hold feasts often. There are very important social reasons behind this custom.

Feasts are usually held when important life events take place, such as a birth, death, marriage, or important birthday. It would be unthinkable and almost a matter of family dishonor should a grandmother's 70th birthday, for example, not be celebrated in this manner.

Besides the pure happiness of celebrating, these feasts are a means by which Kazakhs establish and maintain their social status. A family that is putting on a celebration calls upon its relations and friends to help out, and this help is returned when their friends or other family members have to hold a celebration. Gifts are always exchanged at these events—guests come bearing gifts and are given something in return.

This tradition of feasting and gift giving has put a strain on Kazakhs in times of economic difficulty, especially when the country was trying to find its own independent way in the world. Despite this, Kazakhs know that when they invite people to celebrate, they will be invited in return. And when they give a gift, they will also receive one. Common gift items are clothing or cloth, jewelry, rugs and carpets, household goods, and livestock.

Feasting and the exchange of gifts offer Kazakhs the opportunity to later chat about the party itself and share gossip about what happened there. Many people will still be talking about a great feast months later, discussing gifts that were exchanged and their value.

People gather around for food and drinks at a national holiday celebration in Almaty.

FARMERS IN KAZAKHSTAN

Although some Kazakhs have become farmers, this occupation has not always been respected because farmers in the past were accused of depriving traditional nomads of their grazing lands. Kazakhs have long valued a person's wealth according to the number of animals they possess rather than the value of land, which one had the right to use but did not own.

One issue that many Kazakh farmers are facing is that their farming machinery is aging. As of 2019, this was the case for about 90 percent of machines used for farming in Kazakhstan. Although farm machinery manufacturing is a big industry, buying or leasing equipment is expensive for farmers. To help farmers out, in 2019, the government allocated 65 billion tenge (around 170 million in US dollars) to help farmers pay for new equipment.

INTERNET LINKS

https://www.britannica.com/topic/Kazakh
This article gives information about Kazakh nomads.

https://eurasianet.org/as-kazakhstans-economy-regains-vigor -concerns-shift-to-healthcare
Readers can learn more about Kazakhstan's efforts to reform their health-care system at Eurasianet.org.

https://www.export.gov/article?id=Kazakhstan-Education
This overview explores the country's current educational system, offering statistics about enrollment and information on future development.

https://visitkazakhstan.kz/en/about/78
The Visit Kazakhstan site offers some extra insight on gift giving in Kazakhstan.

RELIGION

Muslim styles of dress, like the ones worn by these women, are becoming more commonplace in cities like Almaty.

8

K AZAKHSTAN BOASTS A VARIETY OF religions practiced by its citizens, but Kazakhs are predominantly Muslim. Over 70 percent of Kazakhs practice Islam, while another 26 percent follow some form of Christianity, especially the teachings of the Russian Orthodox Church. Officially, however, Kazakhstan is a secular, or nonreligious, country. Former president Nazarbayev wanted Kazakhstan to be a model of religious tolerance, and so religions are practiced freely and openly, and this is protected by the constitution.

"Everyone shall have the right to determine and indicate or not to indicate his national, party and religious affiliation."
—Kazakhstan's constitution

THE ARRIVAL OF ISLAM

Islam was introduced to the area in the 8th century, when Arabs invaded the southern part of the country. However, many of the nomads did not become Muslims until the 18th century. The religion was practiced more by those who lived in the cities—mostly the traders—than by the pastoral people who had little knowledge of Islam's teachings and practices. The nomads' contact with Islam probably came from the holy men who traveled the steppes, following the Silk Road. However, when Kazakhstan became part of the communist Soviet Union, all forms of

MUSLIM RITUALS AND BELIEFS

Devout Muslims are not allowed to eat pork, drink alcohol, gamble, or be unkind to others. They also have to say their daily prayers. Muslims must pray five times a day—before dawn, at noon, in the mid-afternoon, after sunset, and before going to bed. When it is time to pray, a man called the muezzin calls the people to prayer. His voice can be heard coming from the mosque five times a day. Muslims bow and face Mecca, the holy city for Muslims, when they pray. On Fridays, they must go to the mosque for prayers. It is mostly the men

Muslims sit on prayer rugs at a mosque in Almaty. Devout Muslims pray five times each day.

who pray at the mosque. When women go, they have a separate place in which to pray. Muslim prayers are usually said in Arabic, the language of the Prophet Muhammad.

religion were discouraged and eventually banned. The government closed down the mosques and religious schools and organizations, and arrested the clergy. Nevertheless, the Muslim clerics continued to operate underground, and the people continued to sympathize with their religious leaders. After the Soviet Union fell apart in 1991, the religious climate improved significantly. Today, Kazakhs are free to practice religions of their choosing or no religion at all.

THE FIVE PILLARS OF ISLAM

A dedicated Muslim must follow the Five Pillars of Islam. The "pillars" are beliefs. They are: the *shahadah* (sha-HAHD-ah), the declaration in Arabic that there is only one God, Allah, and that Muhammad is the messenger of Allah; prayer, or *salat* (sa-LAHT); giving alms, or *zakat* (zah-KART); fasting, or *sawm* (sa-AHM); and making a pilgrimage, or *hajj* (HAHJ). Giving alms, the third pillar, is intended to help the poor. Muslims give zakat once a year to the mosque or a Muslim welfare organization. Fasting is observed for the whole of Ramadan, which is the ninth month of the Islamic calendar. Muslims consider this the

84 Kazakhstan

holy month. During this month, Muslims are not allowed to eat or drink during the day. At night, they may resume these normal activities. Finally, a pilgrimage is required at least once in a person's lifetime to the holy city of Mecca. This is called the hajj.

MUSLIM KAZAKHS TODAY

Although government statistics state that over 70 percent of Kazakhstan's population claims to be Muslim, a large number of these people are not devout. Only about 10 percent of Kazakh Muslims support sharia law, the code by which Muslims must live in order to follow God's wishes. This could be because Kazakhs once followed a nomadic lifestyle, with little need for a central religious force. Truly staunch and devout Muslims make up a small percentage of the population. Although there has been a resurgence of interest in Islam since independence, most Kazakhs today are nominally Muslim and do not go to pray at the mosque. They may celebrate the Muslim festivals, but these celebrations have greater social than religious significance. Only those Kazakhs who are devout and able to afford it go on pilgrimages to Muslim holy places in Central Asia or Saudi Arabia. In the 21st century, more restrictions have been placed on practicing Muslims in Kazakhstan. For instance, in 2016, the traditional head scarf worn by Muslim girls and women was prohibited from being worn in schools. President Nazarbayev also wanted to ban traditional black clothing, facial coverings for women, and altered pants for men, saying these were marks of a growing and potentially dangerous strand of Islam.

While many Muslims in Kazakhstan are devout, others choose a looser interpretation of their core beliefs.

OTHER RELIGIONS IN KAZAKHSTAN

The other dominant religion in the country is Christianity, and most Christians in Kazakhstan today belong to the Russian Orthodox Church. Most of the Orthodox Christians are Russians, Ukrainians, and Slavs. They make up about 26 percent of the population. The main Christian churches in Almaty include the Saint Nicholas Cathedral and the Ascension Cathedral, both Russian

The bright and colorful Ascension Cathedral in Almaty is one of many Russian Orthodox houses of worship in Kazakhstan.

Orthodox. Russian Orthodox Christians in Nur-Sultan might practice their beliefs at the Assumption Cathedral. There are also Protestants in Kazakhstan, mainly Baptists, as well as some Roman Catholics, Jews, and others. Another 2.8 percent of Kazakhs identify as atheists. They do not follow a religion or believe in a higher power.

ANCIENT BELIEFS

Most Kazakhs did not adopt Islam as a religion until the 18th century, and it was not strongly enforced or practiced by those who continued to live a nomadic life. Many nomads who still live in the country today continue to observe pre-Islamic religious practices, such as shamanism, animism, and ancestor worship. These three practices are interrelated. Since traditionally the Kazakhs were pastoral and nomadic and depended on weather and animals for their livelihood, it is easy to understand why these beliefs are upheld even now.

In animism, different spirits are believed to inhabit animals. For the Kazakhs, these are the animals they are close to—sheep, cows, horses, and camels. Spirits are also present in the elements of fire, water, and earth, and may be contacted and asked for help. The nomads offer prayers to the water spirit in times of drought, to the earth spirit to ensure good weather, and to the animal spirits when the health of their livestock is threatened.

One ancient belief many Kazakhs held was that spirits could inhabit animals like camels.

Many Kazakhs are superstitious and will wear charms of holy objects to ward off evil spirits. They believe that it is possible to cast an evil eye on people you hate in order to hurt them. Trips to the graves of holy people and ancestors are made to ask for advice or to receive a blessing.

Because the traditional lifestyle is based on the rearing of animals, many customs and beliefs relate to livestock. Someone wishing another person ill will curse the other person's livestock with poor health. For instance, a Kazakh might curse an enemy in this manner: "May you never own your livestock and be unable to migrate with your people," or "May you have neither horse nor camel, but always have to travel on foot." In the same way, blessings are expressed as an abundance of animals or a wish for their successful fertility. A Kazakh wishing someone well might offer this blessing: "May God bless you with a thousand sheep and lambs." When Kazakhs greet one another, it is considered polite to inquire after the health of the other person's animals—for example, "Are you and your livestock healthy?"

INCREASING RELIGIOUS PARTICIPATION

Since independence, there has been an increase in religious activity. All religious groups have gained a new freedom to practice. Many more people now claim to be religious, and there has been an increase in the number of religious organizations in the country.

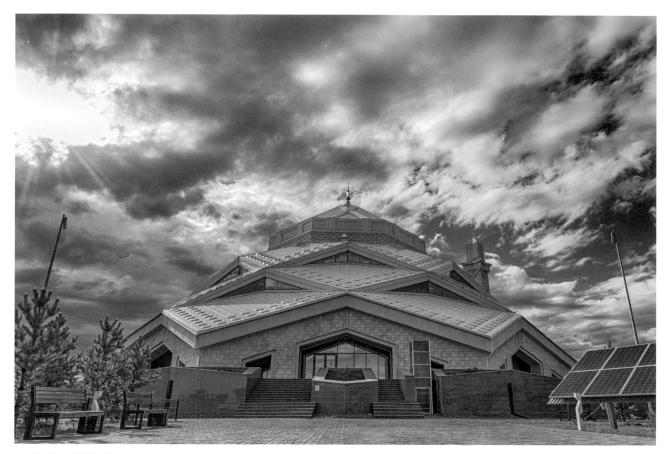

Some groups that were illegal during Soviet times, such as Jehovah's Witnesses and several fundamentalist Christian groups, have been allowed into the country.

Islam is becoming increasingly important in modern Kazakh society. A number of mosques and religious schools have been constructed with financial aid from the Muslim countries of Saudi Arabia, Turkey, and Egypt. In the past, the Nazarbayev government was aware of the potential foreign investment it might receive from the Muslim countries of the Middle East, and for that reason it had been careful to maintain a balance between the Muslim East and the Christian West. When Nazarbayev made a trip to the Muslim holy city of Mecca in 1994, he also visited the Roman Catholic leader, Pope John Paul II, in the Vatican.

From 1985 to 1990, the number of mosques more than doubled, from 25 to 60. An Islamic institute opened in Almaty in 2002. In 2015, the city of Almaty was designated a main Islamic cultural center. Today, there are over 2,000 mosques in the country. In 2018, the Flower of Allah, a new energy-efficient mosque with a modern design, opened in Nur-Sultan.

A SECULAR STATE

Despite the growth of religion since the communist era, Kazakhstan is a secular nation, or one without an official religion. The government hopes that the religious freedom enjoyed in Kazakhstan will serve as a model for other countries, bringing about a kind of peace in Central Asia. Still, Kazakhstan has had its struggles with religious rights, as evidenced by various bans and precautions toward certain styles of Islamic dress.

INTERNET LINKS

https://astanatimes.com/2018/05/kazakh-president-visits-new -mosque-in-futuristic-style
This article provides information on Kazakhstan's new Flower of Allah Mosque and its unusual architecture.

https://www.metmuseum.org/learn/educators/curriculum -resources/art-of-the-islamic-world/unit-one/the-five-pillars -of-islam
Readers can learn more about the Five Pillars of Islam and see some Muslim artworks at the Metropolitan Museum of Art's website.

https://thediplomat.com/2017/07/the-reality-of-religious-freedom -in-kazakhstan
This article featured on the *Diplomat* talks more about religious intolerance in Kazakhstan and how it is on the rise.

LANGUAGE

ШЫМБҰЛАҚ 700м

ЧИМБУЛАК 700м

SHYMBULAK 700m

This sign is written in the three most commonly used languages in Kazakhstan: Russian, Kazakh, and English.

9

THERE ARE TWO OFFICIAL languages in Kazakhstan: Kazakh and Russian. Around 83 percent of Kazakhs speak Kazakh, but a higher percentage (94.4 percent) speak and understand Russian. A little over 22 percent of Kazakhs speak English in addition to the other two languages, making them trilingual, or able to speak three languages fluently. However, as Kazakhstan continues to try to establish its independence from Russia, its relationship with the Russian language may one day become a thing of the past.

When Kazakhstan became independent, the language problem became a contentious one. President Nazarbayev tried to make Kazakh the only official language in the hopes of ensuring its survival as a language. However, Russians in the country were afraid that it would lead to discrimination against them if Kazakh should become the only legal state language. There was also the danger that a strong Kazakh language policy would cause skilled Russians, Slavs, and Germans to leave the country. Ultimately, the government relaxed a little in its language policy, giving Kazakh a special status as the state language while also keeping Russian

In 2011, two Russian schools in the Kazakh city of Temirtau decided to make Kazakh the language teachers would use to communicate with and instruct students. This was happening at a number of places in the country due to Kazakhstan's desire to have the majority of citizens speaking Kazakh by 2020, as well as an influx of Kazakh speakers to the nation and a decline of Russian speakers.

The Temirtau schools' education department made this decision after finding that a number of Russian schools were short on students, while Kazakh schools were overflowing. At the time, several other schools in Temirtau taught in Russian. Still, making the change at the two schools in question would be disruptive for the schools' 1,200 students, forcing them to switch to a different school if they wanted to continue learning in their first language.

Shortly after the announcement was made, 300 people, consisting of teachers, students, and their parents, filed lawsuits against the education department. Teachers who opposed the change were told they would be relocated to other schools; however, in the end, some of them were left without jobs.

as an official language. There are both Kazakh and Russian schools in which the other language is taught as a second language, and Russian is still the main language for certain types of communication. It is the language that helps different ethnic groups in the country communicate with one another. However, efforts are being made to place more of an emphasis on Kazakh. For example, President Nazarbayev banned the use of Russian in official cabinet meetings in 2018, a move that proved challenging for those government ministers who were more fluent in Russian than Kazakh.

THE LANGUAGE OF KAZAKH

Before the 20th century, Kazakh was written with an Arabic script. In 1929, the Latin, or Roman, script was introduced, and in 1940, Cyrillic script was used. Initiated by Joseph Stalin, this alphabet unified the written languages of the Soviet Central Asian republics with that of Russia. Modified in 1954, the 42-letter script used 33 letters of the standard Russian alphabet and some symbols specific to the Kazakh language. In 2018, President Nazarbayev announced that Kazakhstan would be switching to a Latin alphabet by 2025. The transition hasn't been easy, though. The Latin alphabet doesn't have characters for every inflection in the Kazakh language, so linguists continue to puzzle over how to modify the alphabet to compensate.

Kazakh is a Turkic language with strong influences from other historical languages in the region, such as Arabic, Persian, Tatar, and Mongolian. It is part of the Nogai-Kipchak subgroup of northeastern Turkic languages.

Kazakh has several dialects, or versions. The main ones are Northeastern Kazakh, Southern Kazakh, and Western Kazakh. These dialects are quite similar to each other.

This Almaty newsstand is stocked with both Kazakh- and Russian-language newspapers.

KAZAKHSTAN'S MEDIA

The main newspapers in Kazakhstan include the national *Egemen Kazakhstan*, published in Kazakh, and the Russian-language *Kazakhstanskaya Pravda*. The *Astana Times* is run through Kazakhstan's Ministry of Information and is for a global audience.

There are many other newspapers, and although these enjoy a certain amount of freedom of expression, guaranteed in the 1995 constitution, the government has increased control over what is being published, even engaging in outright censorship.

Some private newspapers have been refused publishing facilities at the government presses for various "technical" reasons, and sponsors of newspapers deemed problematic have faced investigations or had financial pressure brought on them. The law explicitly forbids any personal criticism of the president, his family, or other high-level officials.

Several newspapers have political links. The *Respublika* was published by the Socialist Party until it was sold to a commercial enterprise after the Kazakh government worked to shut it down, even taking their fight to the US court

"Language is a very delicate sphere that cannot be dictated by officials."
—Aidos Saraym, Kazakh political analyst

THE WORD "KAZAKH"

The word "Kazakh" was found in a Turkish-Arabic dictionary in 1245. It means "independent, free, wanderer, exile," and according to one of the interpretations, it refers to a free person who broke away from his or her people to lead the life of an adventurer, or to a group of nomads. The nomads in Kazakhstan were originally called Uzbek-Kazakhs because they were members of the Uzbek tribe who had broken away from the group. They began to drop the word "Uzbek" after 1468 when groups of Uzbek-Kazakhs united in victory against the Uzbek tribe. Burunduk Khan (1473–1511) was called the ruler of the "Kazakhs."

Younger Kazakhs may have an easier time than their elders adapting to the Kazakh language as their main language.

system since the company's website ran through an American web host. This type of censorship has become very common in Kazakhstan.

Radio and television are extremely important in linking the distant parts of the country together. Most TV and radio stations in Kazakhstan are owned by the government. People with access to satellite dishes for entertainment can also view foreign media. There are 96 TV channels in the country. Altogether, broadcasts reach about 99 percent of citizens.

THE CHOSEN LANGUAGE

The Kazakh government conducted a study in 1996 to assess the state of the Kazakh language among the people. The study examined how the various ethnic groups viewed and used both Kazakh and Russian.

First of all, it found that the majority of Kazakh people, no matter what ethnic group they belonged to, were effectively bilingual—that is, they could speak their own language and spoke, read, and wrote Russian as their second language. The exceptions were the Russians and the Slavs, who tended to speak only Russian.

KAZAKHS AND THE MOVIES

The first movie studio in Kazakhstan was Vostokkino, which produced documentaries on Soviet policies. A Russian-based studio created a feature film, Amangeldy, *and released it in 1939. The film starred Kazakh actors and told the story of national hero Amangeldy Imanov. World War II relocated the Moscow film studio Mosfilm temporarily to Almaty while the Soviet Union was at war. This gave Kazakh filmmakers an opportunity to make their own movies, and the momentum continued even after the war came to an end in 1945. Kazakh filmmakers continued to make films, and since 1990, over 2,000 private film studios have been established. Film continues to be a growing medium in Kazakhstan.*

Today, more people are speaking Kazakh; however, Russian is still the dominant language. The government is doing more to encourage more Kazakh speakers. Young people are also doing their part.

Older generations who lived during the Soviet era tend to speak Russian, while younger people are learning Kazakh at a younger age. Since half of Kazakhs are under the age of 29 and many are pushing back against the ingrained values of the Soviet era, this could bring big changes for Kazakhstan and its tenuous relationship with language.

INTERNET LINKS

https://www.bbc.com/worklife/article/20180424-the-cost-of -changing-an-entire-countrys-alphabet
This article from the BBC looks at the switch from a Cyrillic to a Latin alphabet for the Kazakh language.

https://www.omniglot.com/writing/kazakh.htm
The language site Omniglot takes a look at the Kazakh language and the various alphabets it has used over the years.

ARTS

10

THE ARTS ARE ALIVE AND THRIVING in Kazakhstan. Kazakh artists are painters and sculptors. Kazakhs enjoy music, theater, books, and more. Much of the arts of Kazakhstan are rooted in its past, but contemporary forms of expression are on the rise. Independence from the Soviet Union has allowed artists to fully express themselves.

"Songs and horses
are the two wings of
the Kazakh people."
—Kazakh proverb

HISTORY THROUGH STORYTELLING

Before the mid-19th century, most Kazakh customs and traditions were passed down through an oral tradition of stories and poetry. Storytellers and singers, called *akyns* (A-keens), and lyric poets, known as *jhyrau* (JAI-rau), were entrusted with the responsibility of memorizing the legends and history of the Kazakh people and keeping their cultural history alive by reciting it and passing it on to the next generation of storytellers.

Akyns were storytellers who traveled from one nomadic camp to another, reciting the epic stories of Kazakh history and legend. Many of the stories tell of the exploits of legendary warriors and their struggle against Mongol Kalmyks. The stories were often recited with the accompaniment of traditional instruments such as the drum. The Kalmyks were pastoral nomads and descendants of the Mongols who lived in the eastern and southeastern parts of the country. They fought the Kazakhs for control of the land in the 17th century.

Older generations of Kazakhs pass down stories of their pasts and stories from generations ago through the oral tradition of storytelling.

However, not all stories tell of battles or warrior heroes. Some are romantic tales, such as the love story of Enlik and Kebek, who choose death in the face of family opposition to their love, while others, such as the most famous love story, *Kyz-Zhibek*, are lyrical love poems.

The poems and poetic songs of the ancient khanate period survived because they were preserved orally until the late 19th century, when Kazakh intellectuals recorded them. However, the Soviets suppressed these records until the 1960s.

The jhyrau were very respected members of their tribes and honored as elders. They were often part of the ruler's group of followers. Unlike the akyns, the jhyrau had contact with the world at large, and their poetry contained Islamic elements with references to Allah.

One famous poet was Asan Kangi, who lived from 1370 to 1465. He served the Mongolian court of the Golden Horde. Other notable poets include Dosbambet Jhyrau (1490—1523) and Jhalkiz Jhyrau (1465—1560).

MUSIC

Music plays a big role in Kazakh life, complementing the oral tradition of storytelling. It is a means of entertainment, and no festival is complete without a band of musicians playing. Together with storytelling, music is also a way of recording tribal history in song, and it has magical qualities when it's employed by the shaman or medicine man.

Unique to the Kazakhs is the musical-oral tradition of *ajtys*. This is a competition requiring the contestants, both men and women, to improvise with poetry and music. Two contestants try to outdo each other in composing the better song.

The nomads used songs and instrumental music called *kujs* to pass on their traditions from one generation to the next. For example, each seasonal migration was blessed by a special song sung by an elder, called the *aksakal*.

A popular Kazakh story is that of a young 17th-century woman, Zhibek, who has been promised to a suitor. However, she and Tulegen, the young chief of the Lesser Horde, meet and fall in love. The rejected suitor then kills Tulegen. In revenge, Zhibek's brother kills the suitor. The story then moves ahead to eight years later, when Sansizbai, Tulegen's younger brother, returns from the war and learns of his brother's death. Zhibek is then about to be married to a Kalmyk prince. Sansizbai kills the prince and escapes with Zhibek. He marries her and thus fulfills his duty and honors the memory of his slain brother. This story is still told today.

There are more than 50 Kazakh musical instruments—string, wind, and percussion. They are made from wood, metal, reed, leather, horn, and horsehair. The most common string instruments that Kazakhs play are the two-stringed, lute-like instrument called the *dombra*, and the *kobyz*, a violin-like instrument with three strings. Some older lutes have strings that are made of horsehair and others of silk. The body of the kobyz is made of one piece of wood, and the strings are played with a bow. Another string instrument is the *zhetigen*, which has a rectangular wooden body and seven strings made of horsehair. It is used mainly as a solo instrument or as an accompanying instrument in folk orchestras and ensembles.

These Kazakh musicians are playing traditional instruments.

The *sybyzgy* is a wind instrument. Commonly used by traditional musicians, it is made of reed or wood and resembles two small wooden flutes put together. The *adyrna* is also a wind instrument. Although it is basically a musical instrument, hunters often use it because the whistle-like sound that it makes resembles the cries of birds and other animals.

There are several percussion instruments. The *dangyra* is similar to the tambourine. One side is covered with leather, and the inner rim of the

Arts **99**

The Focus Kazakhstan art program, run through the National Museum of the Republic of Kazakhstan, wants to bring Kazakh art to the rest of the world. Fine art of Kazakhstan has two distinctive modern eras: pre-independence art, in which artists trained in creating propaganda with a social purpose under the Soviet regime, and post-independence art, which allows artists to truly express themselves and explore modern ideas. At the program's shows in Berlin, Germany, and London, England, in 2018, contemporary Kazakh artists were paired with Soviet-era artists, their works displayed together. This allowed museum visitors to see how Kazakhstan's art has been affected by its journey to independence.

instrument is lined with metal pendants that produce clacking sounds when the instrument is struck. Two drum-like instruments are the *dauylpaz* and the *dabyl*. Both are beaten with the hand or a whip and are often used for signaling in the army and for hunting.

The *asatayak* is used in shamanistic rituals. It is a wooden staff or rod about 3 feet (1 m) long with metal pendants at the top. When shaken, it produces a rattling sound.

Traditional Kazakh folk singers often accompany their performances on the dombra or kobyz. There are many traditional folk songs that are sung on special occasions, such as the *koshtasu*, a song of farewell for close friends and family; the *yestirtu*, sung to announce the death of someone dear; the *zhoktau*, a song of lamentation; and the *konil aitu*, a song to comfort those who are grieving.

The Museum of Kazakh Musical Instruments in Almaty, built in 1907, houses a unique collection of traditional Kazakh musical instruments. It houses exhibits about famous Kazakh musicians and allows visitors the opportunity to engage with an ethno-folk performance group called Turan. On its property also lies a concert hall, where many weddings and musical performances take place. The wooden museum building itself is of artistic and historical interest. It is the achievement of the architect Andrei Zenkov, who built Ascension Cathedral in Almaty, another totally wooden building.

ARTS AND CRAFTS

Kazakh arts and crafts have a long tradition. The people of this country are well known for their beautiful embroidery work on all types of daily and ceremonial articles, such as the velvet vest that is part of the Kazakh traditional dress. Multicolored threads are combined with beads and stones to decorate items made of cloth, leather, felt, and other materials.

Carpet making is another tradition for which Kazakhs are famous. The northeastern part of the country is well known for this craft. Many Kazakh houses are decorated with handmade felt carpets and rugs of intricate colors and geometric designs.

The process of making a felt carpet is elaborate. It begins with the cleaning and dying of the wool. The dyed wool is then laid on a mat of hay and reeds (called *shij*) harvested from the steppes, wet down, and then walked on by everyone in the household. This trampling mats and fuses the wool fibers. The designs are then cut out of different colored felts and combined. This arrangement is then covered by the reed mat and stepped on again until the sections stick to each other. When the carpet is uncovered, the youngest daughter in the family sews everything together.

These two grandmothers and two of their grandchildren spin wool. Decorative woven rugs are displayed in the background.

Since independence, pop music has been on the rise in Kazakhstan. K-pop from Korea and Japanese pop music are both extremely influential, and today many Kazakhs listen to Q-pop (Qazak/Kazakh pop). The Q-pop group Ninety-One formed in 2015 and has huge fan bases in Almaty and Nur-Sultan. The group is made up of five members: A.Z., Alem, Ace, Zaq, and Bala. Their look is often described as "flamboyant" and is a little controversial for more conservative Kazakhs. Adopting a K-pop-influenced look, the group sports dyed hair, makeup, and jewelry. During a tour of Kazakhstan in 2016, the group was met with protesters, demanding that several performances be canceled. Ninety-One continues to record music, however, and they have a growing fan base outside of Kazakhstan.

Silver jewelry has long been popular in Kazakhstan. This piece of jewelry was meant to be worn while riding a horse.

SILVER

Silversmithing as a Kazakh craft reached its height in the late 19th and early 20th centuries. Today, it continues as a livelihood for some. In the past, the silversmiths were kept busy by the wealthy, who required jewelry to complement their ornate costumes. The designs of Kazakh jewelry are similar to those of other Central Asian societies, such as the Turkmen and Tatars. Plant and animal motifs are used widely, as are geometric patterns, including circles, triangles, and dots. The silversmiths are skilled in engraving. Intricate filigree is one of the hallmarks of fine Kazakh jewelry. Delicate lacy designs are created with gold and silver wire. Further ornamentation is achieved by making use of precious and semiprecious stones for color and detail.

PAINTING KAZAKHSTAN

Creativity remains a part of the Kazakh tradition to this day. It manifests in a number of ways, through the many painters, sculptors, folk artists, craftspeople, and other creative people living in the country.

Popular subjects for artists are natural landscapes, especially the steppes; the changing seasons; people in the city and in nomadic settings; and portraits of famous Kazakhs.

Abylkhan Kasteyev (1904—1973) is a well-known artist and is recognized as a pioneer of Kazakh painting. He painted idealized images of collectivization and the Virgin Lands program. Among his major works are the paintings *A Hunter with a Golden Eagle*, *An Alpine Skating Rink*, and *Summer Pasture of Chalkude*. Two other artistic influences are sculptor Khakimzhan Naurzbayev (b. 1925) and painter, cinema artist, and theater artist Gulfairus Ismailova (1929—2013). Several of Naurzbayev's monuments to famous Kazakhs can be found in the city of Almaty. Ismailova's works include the film setting for the Kazakh epic love story *Kyz-Zhibek*. She also created stage sets for classic operas like *Aida* by Giuseppe Verdi, *Iolanta* by Pytor Tchaikovsky, and *The Czar's Bride* by Nikolai Rimsky-Korsakov.

The yellow exterior of the Abay Kazakh State Academic Opera and Ballet Theatre makes it hard to miss.

MUSEUMS AND THE THEATER

Almaty is a lively center of Kazakh art and culture, with many theaters and museums. The Abay Kazakh State Academic Opera and Ballet Theatre, which was established in 1934, stages Kazakh operas and ballets, as well as Western productions. In 2018, it took its one-act ballet productions of *Chopiniana* and *Scheherazade* abroad, performing in France and later at the Coliseum in London, England. There are also theaters that showcase the artistic traditions of other communities in the country, such as the Korean State Musical Comedy Theater. The Korean Theater, originally formed in Vladivostok in 1932, arrived in Kyzylorda in 1937, when Koreans were deported by the Russians to Kazakhstan; the theater was moved to Almaty in 1968, where it still exists today.

Kazakhs love museums. The Central State Museum in Almaty is the city's largest museum. It houses a permanent collection of archaeological finds from all over the country. These include historical artifacts relating to ancient, modern, and natural history and the history of the major ethnic

This sculpture of Abay Kunanbayev stands in Uralsk, in the northwestern region of Kazakhstan.

"A strong man may defeat one hundred enemies. But a learned man— one thousand." —Abay Kunanbayev

communities in the country. Almaty is also home to the A. Kasteyev State Museum of Arts, which was established in 1935 with a beginning collection of almost 200 artworks by Russian and European artists. Today, it also has a section of traditional Kazakh crafts, jewelry, and clothing, as well as Chinese, European, and Kazakh paintings. Other museums in Almaty include the Archaeology Museum, Geology Museum, Nature Museum, and even the Museum of Books.

KAZAKH WRITERS

Abay Kunanbayev (1845—1904), also known as Abai Qunanbaiuly, or simply Abai, is probably the best-known literary figure in Kazakh history. He was born in the Chingiz-Tau Mountains, south of the town of Semey in northeastern Kazakhstan. Although Kunanbayev never left his native land, he was very well educated and knowledgeable about the world. He spoke several languages, among them Russian, Arabic, and Persian. Kunanbayev spent three years in an Islamic school, then taught, translated Russian literature into Kazakh, and wrote poetry. He was a nationalist who promoted Kazakh cultural identity. He spoke out strongly for the need to educate the young in order to create a moral and spiritual world. Kunanbayev idealized the traditional Kazakh life, while also advocating progress through collaboration with the Russians. Through his work, Kazakh earned its place as a literary language.

Mukhtar Auezov (1897—1961) was the son of a nomadic family. He was a writer, literary critic, historian, and linguist. Through his writings, he gave immortality to the life and culture of his people and country. He learned the power of the written word early in life. As a child, he was amazed to discover that Kazakh stories and songs could be written and preserved on paper. His greatest book is the epic called *The Path of Abay*, or *Abay's Way*. In it he explores the life and philosophy of the poet Abay Kunanbayev, paying homage to the poet he revered above all others. Auezov died at the age of 64 in Moscow.

Modern writers in Kazakhstan are gaining fame as well. Kazakh novelist, poet, and journalist Saule Doszhan was honored for her work in 2015, named Honored Art Worker of Kazakhstan for that year. Her novel *My Own Strange Heart* told a fictionalized account of the first heart transplant performed by Kazakh surgeons in 2012. This book and her later work *The Tragedy of a Bastard* were translated into Russian and English.

Visitors examine a colorful mural in the Almaty metro station named for one of Kazakhstan's most famous writers, Mukhtar Auezov.

INTERNET LINKS

https://astanatimes.com/2018/12/poet-saule-doszhan-introduces -kazakh-life-stories
Learn more about contemporary writer Saule Doszhan in this article.

https://www.youtube.com/channel/UCd3X-p_3fRLHnu8LCPOMTNg
Viewers can check out some of Ninety-One's hits on the group's YouTube channel.

https://www.youtube.com/watch?v=f-BUf3fOX6E
Kazakh folk dancers performed for the International Festival of Language and Culture in 2016, as shown here.

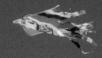

LEISURE

Kazakh families enjoy some fun and kite flying in front of the Hazrat Sultan Mosque in Nur-Sultan.

11

K AZAKHSTAN HAS MUCH TO DO FOR fun and enjoyment. Some popular activities involve horses. Children learn to ride at a young age, and riding a horse in Kazakhstan may be considered as commonplace as riding a bike in America. More than just sources of leisure, however, horses have been very important to Kazakhs throughout the country's history. In fact, evidence of some of the earliest domestic horses has been found in Kazakhstan, suggesting that ancient Kazakhs both rode horses and prized them for their milk.

THE GAME OF COURTSHIP

There are a number of traditional games that Kazakhs play on horseback. One is a catch-me-if-you-can game of tag that boys and girls sometimes play. It is called *kyz kuu* (KISS-ku), or "overtake the girl." When a boy catches a girl, he wins a kiss from her. If he doesn't catch her, then she gets to hit him with her riding whip.

GETTING THE GOAT

Kokpar is a very popular game in Kazakhstan, but not for someone with a weak stomach. It is a wild, free-for-all scramble by Kazakhs on horseback who fight for possession of the carcass of a goat. Perhaps the game that is most similar to kokpar is polo, also called *shogen*. The chase on horseback is the same, but there the similarity ends. In kokpar, instead of a polo ball, the headless carcass of a goat is tossed around. As many as 1,000 participants can take part in the chase. There are no boundaries; the action can extend out over the steppes. The game supposedly originated as a sacrificial tradition where a goat was killed in order to obtain the blessings of the spirits. After the game, there would be a grand feast and musical performances.

The horses ridden by ancient Kazakh nomads needed to be capable of carrying a rider for long distances, often over very rough terrain. The alaman baiga *is a horse race that tests this type of endurance. The race is a long-held tradition, originally a serious test of endurance—but today the alaman baiga is held for entertainment. The original races required riders and their horses to travel up to 62 miles (100 km) over the ground, but today the races are limited to about 19 miles (30 km) and are usually held in stadiums with large crowds. Shorter races are also popular. These races are held on level ground and only go up to 5.6 miles (9 km). Riders in these races are often young boys, between 8 and 14 years of age. In 2014, a 12-year-old boy and his horse won the Altyn Tulpar alaman baiga.*

KUMIS ALU

Another time-honored game that tests one's horsemanship is *kumis alu*, which means "pick up the coin." The aim is for the rider to gallop at top speed and simultaneously pick up a silver coin from the ground. This game requires the participant to possess almost perfect riding skills. Kazakh folklore says that Alexander the Great, after seeing an exhibition of kumis alu, was so impressed that he exclaimed the game could be used in the training of a warrior on horseback. In modern games, a white handkerchief is used instead of a coin.

The sport of *audaryspak*, or wrestling while on horseback, requires endrance, strength, cunning, and excellent riding skills.

WRESTLING ON HORSEBACK

Kazakhs love wrestling. This sport has a strong Central Asian tradition, and a champion wrestler is an honored man. *Audaryspak*, or wrestling on horseback, pits both riders and their horses in close combat. The winner is the one who is able to unseat his opponent from his horse.

Evidence of polo's origins has been discovered in ancient Turkic writings. Texts such as Kutagu Bilig *and* Divani Lugat al-Turk *seem to depict the game. Historians believe, based on this evidence, that polo originated with nomadic people in Central Asia. It came to Persia as early as the sixth century BCE, and from there it traveled to the Arab world. It thereafter spread to wherever the Arabs went—including India, China, and eventually Europe. The first European polo club was established in the 1860s. This elite game, considered a tradition in Britain, was invented by nomads, perhaps even Kazakh nomads. It has popularity around the world—even royalty play it!*

HUNTING

The sport of hunting with golden eagles has made Kazakhs famous. *Berkutchi* is the name of the sport and also of the men who capture the eagles and teach them to hunt. Eagles are caught in a net trap that is baited with a small animal such as a hare. When an eagle takes the bait and flies into the net, the hunter's first job is to tie the bird's legs together to immobilize its claws. Then, a small leather hood is thrown over its eyes. This usually calms the bird. Next, the patient job of training the bird starts.

The hood is kept on the eagle while it becomes accustomed to the sounds, touch, and presence of people. After a week, the bird is taught to take its food directly from its master's hand. As training progresses, the eagle is given more freedom and is allowed to fly. The bond between bird and master grows, until finally the eagle can be released and trusted to return when called. The master uses stuffed foxes to train the eagle to hunt.

Berkutchi hunt for foxes with an eagle and a horse. They ride on the steppes in search of a fox. When one is spotted, the hunter takes off the leather hood covering the bird's eyes and launches the bird into the sky. As the eagle circles in the sky and then swoops down on its prey, the hunter follows closely on his horse. The eagle catches the fox in its strong talons. The hunter has to be quick to call his bird back, rewarding its success with some raw meat he keeps in a little leather pouch. The hood is quickly slipped back on to calm down the bird.

In Kazakhstan, like in Chinese culture, each year is named after an animal—there is the Year of the Sheep, the Year of the Horse, Dog, Snake, Pig, and so on. The year that begins it all is the Year of the Mouse.

Hunters can earn good money by selling fox skins. Fox hunting is a skill that is passed down from father to son, but it is a dying tradition in the 21st century. More frequently, hunters display their skills in events at festivals or for tourists who visit the country. Regardless, it remains one of the oldest sports in Kazakhstan. Petroglyph drawings of men hunting with an eagle testify to its long history.

Besides golden eagles, hunters sometimes use hawks and falcons. They also hunt other birds, such as partridges, ducks, and pigeons, and animals, such as hares and even wolves.

Storytelling, often with the accompaniment of a musical instrument, became an important pastime and continues to have value today.

TELLING STORIES

Storytelling is an important part of Kazakh tradition, going back to the days when the akyn, or storyteller, would journey from camp to camp to tell stories. The akyn would tell of the people's history or sing songs. Both adults and children looked forward to a visit from the akyn.

The stories were a means of remembering the history of the Kazakhs and of teaching social values. Many stories had morals to teach, and they were often about the animals of the steppes. However, these animals were endowed with human characteristics. For instance, Mouse is small but intelligent and outwits the bigger and stronger animals. Kazakh children all know about Aldar Kose, a clever and witty character who gets the better of others who are greedy or selfish by exploiting their failings. Aldar Kose is very much like Coyote, the trickster animal in some Native American folktales.

MODERN LEISURE ACTIVITIES

Sports and other outdoor leisure activities are popular in Kazakhstan. The Medeu Alpine Sports Center near Almaty is a popular place for winter sports.

It has the world's highest ice-skating rink, at 5,548 feet (1,691 m) above sea level. Likewise, its rink is one of the world's longest, at 1,313 feet (400 m) long. During the winter, it is enjoyed by ice hockey teams, world-class speed skaters, and the public. Hundreds of skaters can be seen swirling and tumbling across the ice. It is the site for many international competitions, and more than 100 world skating records have been broken there. The complex also gives visitors the opportunity to partake in other sports, such as skiing. In the summer, it is open to mountain bikers and hikers.

Hunting and fishing are also popular activities in the country. Foxes, wolves, deer, wild boar, and birds such as partridges and pheasants are all popular game. Fishing enthusiasts like to catch roach, carp, chub, and silverfish. A government license is required for fishing and hunting.

The country also offers numerous spas that are popular with both residents and tourists. These holiday resorts offer guests all sorts of medicinal treatments with curative waters.

In Almaty's Panfilov Park, Kazakh men play chess in the shadow of Ascension Cathedral. Chess is an extremely popular game among Central Asians and has been for a very long time.

Kazakhs are becoming increasingly exposed to modern culture from around the world. Movie theaters and television networks show American, Russian, Chinese, and Turkish movies. Over 2 million residents have access to broadband internet, and streaming services such as Netflix are getting a foothold in the region. Citizens also enjoy attending rock concerts and nightclubs in busier cities such as Almaty and Nur-Sultan.

INTERNET LINKS

https://aboutkazakhstan.com/blog/travel/medeu-a-unique-high -altitude-skating-rink
The Medeu Alpine Sports Center is impressive in itself, but its mountainous backdrop is even more captivating. Here, read all about the skating rink and its scenery.

https://silkadv.com/en/content/alaman-baiga
Readers can see photos of an alaman baiga race at the Silk Road Adventures website.

FESTIVALS

Kazakh children in traditional dress
celebrate Constitution Day in 2016.

12

I N KAZAKHSTAN, HOLIDAYS SERVE AS A reminder of significant social and political moments, such as Constitution Day, which marks the day Kazakhstan's constitution was officially adopted following independence. There's also an Independence Day, celebrated in December, to commemorate the day Kazakhstan became independent. Women's Day, Victory Day, and Defender of the Fatherland Day are also popular times. Regardless of the holiday, there are special traditions and events associated with it.

There are no official religious holidays as such, but both Christmas and the Muslim Eid al-Adha (called Kurban Ait in Kazakh) are days when no one is expected to work, thus making them essentially holidays. Eid al-Adha is a time of sacrifice. It remembers when the religious figure Ibrahim nearly sacrificed his son, Isaac, to signal his devotion to Allah. Nauryz, the traditional Central Asian celebration of spring, was added to the Kazakh state calendar in 2001. For Kazakhs, it is a time of unity and celebration of life. Many parades, social gatherings, concerts, and theatrical performances take place to commemorate the holiday.

"Every year we mark our independence with a day of celebration, a milestone to remember how far our nation has come and to acknowledge our future direction."
— *Astana Times* editorial, 2019

CELEBRATIONS DURING SOVIET RULE

Although there was a suppression of Kazakh culture and tradition during Soviet times, the authorities could never really stop the feasts that accompanied the celebrations of life events in the community. Feasting and gift giving have always had great cultural significance in Kazakh society. They create ties that bind people to one another. Today, now that Kazakhstan is independent, Kazakhs are able to celebrate their traditions freely, although many Russian traditions remain and have become part of the celebrations.

NAURYZ

Nauryz is probably the most important festival of the year, celebrated by everyone in Kazakhstan, regardless of their ethnicity. It is a celebration of the coming of spring, the emergence of the first grain or sheaf of wheat, the lambing season, and the first milking. The festival is also called "the first day of the New Year" or "the great day of the people."

Symbols that are associated with Nauryz are the color white, which stands for goodness and riches; sweets, for abundance; and the number seven, which has a mystical significance. The traditional Nauryz dish is *kozhe*, made with seven kinds of grain, including rice, millet, and wheat. The elders of the family are ceremonially offered seven bowls of kozhe.

No effort is spared in this celebration, since Kazakhs believe that the more one celebrates Nauryz, the greater one's reward and success for the rest of the year will be. A lot of cooking, especially of special dishes that symbolize abundance and good tidings, is done as people visit family and friends to wish them well in the coming year. It is important that there is more than enough food and drink for all.

Although Nauryz was originally a nonreligious celebration with Persian origins, it has been given a Muslim flavor in the southern part of the country. The celebrations are blessed by the Muslim imam and presided over by the elders of the community. Celebrations begin when the New Year is greeted at noon with a prayer honoring the ancestors. This is read by the religious

Colorfully dressed girls dance as part of the Nauryz celebration in the city of Shymkent.

leader. Then, the eldest in the family solemnly gives a blessing and wishes of prosperity and goodwill to everybody present.

Entertainment during Nauryz blends the modern with the traditional. In the cities, Nauryz has a more secular nature. Processions, with horsemen dressing up as Kazakh heroic warriors, fill the streets, while wrestling competitions and horse races bring an air of excitement. Musicians perform for a lively audience, and folk singers engage in song battles.

The atmosphere during Nauryz resembles that of a carnival. In addition to the entertaining variety shows, there are stalls selling food and all kinds of merchandise.

MUSLIM HOLIDAYS AND CELEBRATIONS

Kazakh Muslims, like their counterparts elsewhere, observe Ramadan, the ninth month of the Islamic year, and the feast of Eid al-Fitr, also called Little Bairam

THE HISTORY OF NAURYZ

The celebration of Nauryz came to Kazakhstan through the influence of the nearby Persians many centuries ago. It is still celebrated in Iran, modern-day Persia, where it is called No Ruz or Norooz, which means "new day" in the Farsi, or Persian, language. In Kazakhstan, Nauryz is a celebration of the coming of spring and the symbolic victory of good over evil. The first No Ruz was believed to have been celebrated by the legendary Persian emperor Jamshid. Some historians think it was celebrated as long ago as in the 12th century BCE. Since Nauryz is a time for renewal, families clean their homes to remove the previous year's dust, open their homes to everyone, buy new clothes, and visit their friends.

Muslim women offer snacks outside a mosque in Nur-Sultan on Eid al-Adha.

or the Festival of the Breaking of the Fast, which marks the end of Ramadan. The next important Muslim celebration is Eid al-Adha, also called the Great Festival or the Festival of the Sacrifice.

Islam follows the lunar calendar, and therefore the feasts are "movable"—that is, their dates change on the Western (solar) calendar from year to year. The first day of the month is determined by the observation of the moon by the religious authority. When the new moon of the ninth month is sighted, Ramadan begins. The holy month ends when the next new moon is seen.

During Ramadan, Muslims fast from sunrise to sunset, abstaining from food, drink, and tobacco, although they still carry on their normal activities. When the month is over, the end of Ramadan is celebrated with the feast of Eid al-Fitr, which usually lasts for three days. During this time, everyone's house is open to all friends and family. People go visiting, and there is a lot to eat and drink.

Eid al-Adha is the Feast of Sacrifice and celebrates the completion of a hajj, or a holy pilgrimage to Mecca, which is the holy city for all Muslims. Families and friends visit one another on this festival.

VICTORY DAY

Victory Day is celebrated every May 9 or 10, commemorating the day in 1945 that Nazi Germany surrendered to the Soviet Union at the end of World War II. Every year, military parades are held to honor the Kazakh soldiers who died fighting in the war, as well as all veterans. Of the 1.8 million Kazakh soldiers who fought for the Soviet army, 600,000 Kazakhs died. On Victory Day in Nur-Sultan, people lay flowers at an eternal flame monument. There are concerts, and musicians play wartime songs. There is lots of food. The celebration is a somber but special occasion in Kazakhstan.

CELEBRATING WITH FEASTS

A little Kazakh boy takes part in feasting in Almaty.

There are many events in a Kazakh's life that call for a feast. Births, deaths, marriages, significant birthdays—these are all celebrated with feasting, songs, and games. There are also many ceremonies for celebrating the special moments in a baby's life—when they are born, the first time they are placed on a bed, when they first stand, when they first walk, and when they are weaned.

The *kyrkynan shygaru* is a feast held to mark a baby's 40 days, when the child is ritually bathed and has their hair and nails cut. Before this time, the young infant is only seen by the immediate family. Now, they become a member of the larger community. *Tusau kesu* marks the time when the baby first starts to walk. The baby's feet are specially tied, and a woman is chosen to cut these ties to signify this milestone in the baby's life.

Boys are often circumcised when they are between five and eight years old. It is common for a boy to be circumcised with other boys, such as his brothers or cousins. There is usually a small gathering and celebration on the day of circumcision. About a month later, a bigger feast is held.

In Kazakhstan, preparations for a celebration begin months before the actual date. Shopping trips to the nearest city are made to buy all the items needed. Wealthy families may travel to the big cities to buy special or hard-to-get foods and gifts. Invitations are printed and sent. Gifts for the guests are picked out and set aside.

Everyone in the family is involved in the preparation. Besides the members of the immediate family, the services of friends and members of the extended family are called on. If possible, the feast is held in the yard. Tables are set up, and animals are slaughtered. Food is cooked over several days.

On the big day itself, guests arrive with their gifts. Gifts can range from a small piece of clothing or jewelry to a camel or a horse. As the guests are shown to their seats, a master of ceremonies begins to take charge of the events of the day. The table of honor is usually the one farthest away from the entrance. This is where the person whom the feast honors sits, together with other important guests. Everyone wears his or her best clothes, whether in traditional attire or in Western dresses and suits.

If it is a wedding, the bride and groom are ushered to their seats by dancers. If it is a circumcision ceremony, then the boy is brought to the guests to be congratulated. The tables are loaded with drinks that usually include an endless flow of hot tea in addition to other beverages. Snacks of nuts, fruit, cookies, and candy keep everyone happy in between the main courses of soup, dumplings, pies, fried dough, and bread. Meat is present in every dish, and the richer the family, the more meat there will be. Sometimes a band is hired to provide some music. Guests listen and dance to the music, and token gifts are presented to the guests who dance best or sing well. Horse races and other games are also part of the festivities, and again, the host family will have gifts to present to the winners of these games.

THE FESTIVALS OF TODAY

Visitors to Kazakhstan can enjoy music and cultural festivals being held all over the country. Almaty, which is alive with the arts, celebrates an International Jazz Festival in the summer with performers from all over the world. Four E, a New Age music and arts festival, takes place in the Almaty area every year, complete with yoga sessions, dancing, concerts, and workshops. The entire weekend focuses on the "four Es" of ecology, ethnic culture, emotions, and evolution. Also in Almaty, which means "the place with the apples," Kazakhs celebrate with an apple festival each year.

In Nur-Sultan, a Turkic music festival, the Spirit of Tengri, has helped revive interest in Turkic songs. Participants come from all the Central Asian Turkic-speaking nations. They perform shamanic chants, practice throat singing, sing epic compositions, and play songs on traditional instruments. As part of the Unity Day celebrations on May 1, Nur-Sultan also hosts a festival meant to build friendships among the people of Kazakhstan.

INTERNET LINKS

http://4e.kz/en
Explore more about the Four E festival at this English version of its website.

https://www.qppstudio.net/publicholidays2019/kazakhstan.htm
Readers can see a full list of Kazakhstan's public holidays via this website, as well as the public holidays of other countries.

https://traveltriangle.com/blog/festivals-in-kazakhstan
Travelers to Kazakhstan can learn more about festivals at the Travel Triangle website.

FOOD

Preparing good food and treating guests with honor is an important part of the culinary tradition in Kazakhstan. This Kazakh woman proudly prepares a meal.

13

• • • • • • • • • • • • •
"Konak keldi-irisyn
ala keldi." ("The
guest comes and
brings happiness to
the home.")
—Popular Kazakh
saying

ENTERTAINING OTHERS AND EATING food are extremely important in Kazakhstan. Any special occasion is an excuse for celebration, be it a wedding, a new baby, or even just new neighbors. Guests are treated with the utmost hospitality when visiting a Kazakh home. The food they are served is varied and plentiful. Guests bring a nice gift and are given a place of honor—the *tor*, or head of the table. They receive the best cuts of meat. There is laughter and sometimes a game of cards at the end. Everyone ends the night full and happy.

POPULAR CUISINE

Many different types of food are available in Kazakhstan—not only Kazakh, but also Russian, Georgian, Uzbek, Korean, German, Chinese, Thai, and French. Japanese and Mexican foods, like sushi and tacos, are slowly finding a foothold in Kazkahstan. Pizza and hamburgers are pretty easy to find in Nur-Sultan and Almaty. Kazakhs pride themselves on the cosmopolitan and varied cuisine available in their cities. However, locals might tell visitors that the best food to be found is the traditional type served in the Kazakh home. Home cooking is prized above all other types of food.

MEAT AND FISH

Meat is the most important feature of any Kazakh dinner. Although Kazakhs eat a lot of beef and mutton, or sheep, horse meat is prized above all and is often reserved for very special dishes. Almost all parts of the animal are eaten, including the internal organs. Horse meat also has international appeal. In 2019, Kazakhstan began negotiating the shipment of horse meat to Japan, to be used in a specialty raw horse meat dish there.

Kazy, *zhuzhyk*, *zhaya*, *zhal*, and *karta* are all delicacies made from horse flesh. They are all either salted or smoked and boiled. Kazy is a sausage made of smoked meat taken from the horse's ribs. It is salted, peppered, spiced, and put into horse intestines that have been washed and cleaned in salt water. It is

Kazakhs enjoy meaty dishes. The Green Bazaar in Almaty sells meat for all occasions.

Superstition remains a big part of Kazakh culture, and some of this involves food and eating. There are many beliefs about which parts of the animal may be eaten. For instance, young men are given the ears because it will make them attentive; young girls get the palate to make them more diligent. Children may not eat the brain of the animal for fear that it might make them weak-willed, and young girls are never given the elbow for fear they may not marry.

Children are often taught not to eat from knives, since knives were used for rituals in ancient times and might be dangerous. Refrigerators should remain closed, and kitchen cleanup after a meal is important because a dirty kitchen may attract bad spirits.

Many of these beliefs have disappeared over the years, written off as silly or simply forgotten. However, parents continue to pass down certain beliefs to their children today.

sometimes served sliced with hot noodles. Zhuzhyk is another kind of dried or smoked sausage. Zhaya is made from the meat of the horse's hip. Zhal is the fat from the underpart of the horse's neck. Karta is made from the horse's intestine. It is carefully washed without removing the fat and turned inside out, dried, smoked, and salted.

Shashlyk, or kebabs, are pieces of mutton and fat skewered and barbecued over a charcoal stove. They are often sold at street stalls.

Fish and chicken are also part of the Kazakh diet but are not as important as beef, mutton, and horse meat. Fish comes mainly from the Caspian Sea and includes pike, perch, sprat, sturgeon, and salmon. It is usually boiled but is sometimes fried. Boiled chicken and fried fish can be served as cold appetizers before the main meat dish is presented. Caviar is a delicacy in Kazakhstan.

THE ELEMENTS OF KAZAKH CUISINE

Kazakh cuisine is varied. Rice, vegetables, legumes, milk products, and bread are commonly eaten. Vegetables are always part of a meal, but they are seldom the main course. Radishes, carrots, potatoes, onions, peppers, and various types of green vegetables are often accompaniments to meat dishes. Kazakhs like their food spiced and garnished with garlic, dill, parsley, and other herbs. *Plov*, or pilaf, is a rice dish and can be a simple concoction of rice, chopped mutton, and shredded vegetables fried in a large pan. A chef's version would be a fragrant combination of meat and rice, flavored with raisins and other dried fruit and the famous Kazakh apples. *Sorpa* is a soup flavored with meat or fish and served with flour dumplings or rice. *Kespe* is a soup made of meat or poultry and noodles. It is rather oily because Kazakhs love to eat the fatty parts of the meat.

BREADS

Kazakh bread is mainly in the form of flat cakes made with wheat flour, sometimes leavened with yeast. Some breads, such as the *taba-nan*, are baked in an oven or buried in hot charcoal. *Baursaki* are balls of bread dough fried in oil. These are eaten as snacks, with sour cream and sugar, or as an accompaniment to the main meat course. *Lepeshka* is a round, unleavened bread.

Millet, a fine grain, is another important part of the Kazakh diet. It is either ground or used whole. Kazakhs are very inventive in their methods of cooking millet: frying it in fat, boiling it in milk, or adding it to a meat and vegetable soup to create a nourishing broth.

DAIRY

A large and important part of Kazakh cuisine consists of food made of milk and milk products. Kazakhs use the milk of all their livestock—cows, sheep, camels, horses, and goats. Those who live in the country are able to make their own butter, sour cream, yogurt, and cheese. In addition, they produce many other kinds of dairy products.

The milk of an animal that has just had its young is called beestings. This milk is higher in protein and vitamins and lower in sugar and fats than milk produced later. Kazakhs differentiate three kinds of beestings. The milk immediately after calving is black beestings; the milk obtained after the calf has had its first feeding is yellow beestings; and the milk obtained 24 hours after calving is white beestings. Yellow beestings is mixed with milk, poured into a cleaned animal's stomach, and boiled with meat. White beestings is collected in a bucket, boiled, and drunk.

Irimshik is the dried curd made from the milk of a cow, sheep, or goat. Fresh milk is curdled by the addition of a rennet bag. (Rennet comes from the stomachs of animals such as cows and is used to thicken cheese and other dairy products.) The sour milk is then boiled over a low fire until the curds and whey are separated. The curd is then strained and dried in the wind and sun. It has an orange color. The whey can also be boiled slowly until a thick, viscous mass is left at the bottom of the pot. This is cooled and dried in flat sheets, producing *sarysu*. *Sarysu* is sometimes called Kazakh chocolate because it supposedly tastes like chocolate.

BEVERAGES

Kazakhs make a number of drinks from the milk of their animals. Horse and camel milk are served at wedding feasts. *Kymyz* is an alcoholic drink made from fermented mare's milk. It is a traditional drink of the nomads of Central Asia and is extremely popular. The time honored way of making kymyz is to put the mare's milk into a bag made of camel or goat skin, place it in a warm spot in the yurt, and allow the natural fermentation process to take place. This usually occurs within a day. The kymyz is then beaten with a stick.

Shubat is fermented camel's milk. It is richer and fattier than kymyz. Shubat is made in a similar manner, and it must be stirred. *Airan* is a kind of yogurt produced from sheep's, goat's, or mare's milk.

Kazakhs believe in the medicinal and curative qualities of these milk drinks. Besides nutritional value, the drinks are believed to cure a number of digestive and intestinal problems. It is a special honor to be offered any of these drinks, so it would be a social error for a guest to refuse. Guests are often asked to bless a freshly killed lamb. The spirit of the animal is asked permission to partake of its flesh, after which the meat is boiled or smoked and served with flat flour cakes and milk drinks, such as kymyz.

The drink that is most often found at any Kazakh meal is tea. Black tea from India and Sri Lanka is preferred to the cheaper loose, brick tea that comes from China. Brick tea is made from compressed tea leaves. The brick form makes it easier to transport and store. There are many kinds of brick tea; the poorest has twigs and impurities mixed with the tea leaves. The Kazakhs drink tea all the time, both as a thirst quencher and to wash down their food. Green tea is popular in the southern regions of the country, where it is drunk plain without sugar or milk. Only girls and young women can pour the tea, a responsibility that seems simple but really is not. They must ensure that the tea bowls are always full and that there are no tea leaves swimming in the tea. Even if a guest protests that they have had enough to drink, it is still poor hospitality to leave their tea bowl unfilled. The hostess must offer them a *sui-ayak*, or tea bowl of honor.

Coffee, although not as popular as tea, is also a common drink. Sweet black coffee is the norm. A stronger coffee, much like Turkish coffee, is sometimes made by bringing the coffee to a boil a few times in a small coffee pot. Each time the coffee boils, it is quickly taken off the fire, and a cold metal utensil like a spoon is put in it to cool down the drink. This aromatic brew is served in small cups; glasses of cold water are served on the side to wash down the coffee.

BE OUR GUEST

The ultimate in Kazakh hospitality is the *dastarkhan*, a centuries-old tradition of receiving and serving guests. It begins with tea, often accompanied with cream, butter, jam, dried and fresh fruit, nuts, cakes, and other sweets, followed by appetizers that are usually some form of horse flesh and mutton, and vegetable tidbits.

The highlight of the dastarkhan is the *beshbarmak*, or a mixed dish of vegetables, meat, and noodles. It is enjoyed at most special meals and has a long history, stretching back into ancient times. The tradition used to be that guests eating would do so with their hands. A nickname for the meal is "five fingers," to signify this tradition.

Guests are often served separate bowls of rich, fragrant, meaty sorpa. Sometimes kespe is also served. Warm noodles are placed on a plate, and a gravy of meat and vegetables is poured over them.

Finally, a dessert is served to guests. Hosts might serve some baursaki. The fried dough is sprinkled with sugar, similar to American doughnuts. *Chak chak* is a fried honey cake that is popular in Russia and is still served in many Kazakh homes today. Apples and pears may also make an appearance. Dessert is often served with tea and kymyz.

INTERNET LINKS

http://www.foodbycountry.com/Kazakhstan-to-South-Africa/Kazakhstan.html
Read more about food culture in Kazakhstan on the Food in Every Country website.

https://theculturetrip.com/asia/kazakhstan/articles/insider-s-guide-to-the-10-best-restaurants-in-almaty
The Culture Trip website offers a guide on the best restaurants in Almaty.

SORPA

2 pounds mutton on the bone (pork or beef can be subbed if necessary)

1 9-ounce package of egg noodles

2 medium onions (chop one, leave one whole)

1 medium tomato, whole

2 tablespoons salt

1 teaspoon allspice

1 tablespoon whole black peppercorns

3 bay leaves

4 scallions, chopped

½ cup greens (spinach, kale, or mustard greens, chopped)

Place meat (still on the bone) into a large cooking pot. Fill with enough water to cover the meat completely. Add the peppercorns, bay leaves, allspice, and salt. Bring to a boil over a high heat. As the water boils, it will produce foam. Carefully, using a spoon, remove the foam until the broth is clear.

Cover the pot, and let it boil on medium heat for 90 minutes. (If the pot boils over, turn down to low heat.) The meat should be a little bit tender and beginning to separate from the bones.

At this point, add the tomato (whole) and the whole onion. Re-cover, and cook on medium heat for another 30 minutes.

Remove the meat, bones, tomato, and onion, using a sturdy slotted spoon, leaving only the broth in the pot. Set these aside on a plate for now. (You can discard the bay leaves.) Add noodles to the broth. Cook on low heat until the noodles are soft.

While the broth is cooking, separate the meat from the bones and chop into bite-sized pieces, along with the stewed onion and tomato. Chop the remaining onion into small pieces and combine in a separate bowl with the greens of your choice and scallions.

To serve your *sorpa*, pour some broth and noodles into a large soup bowl, add pieces of meat, and then add the onions, tomatoes, scallions, and greens. Add salt to taste, and enjoy!

BAURSAKI (KAZAKH FRIED DOUGH)

4 cups all-purpose flour
2 tablespoons yeast
½ cup warm (not hot) water
½ cup warm (not hot) milk
2 eggs (room temperature)
2 tablespoons unsalted butter (room temperature)
½ tablespoon sugar
½ teaspoon salt
Vegetable oil for frying
Granulated sugar for sprinkling

To get a good rise out of yeast breads, it may be helpful to mix your ingredients in a large glass mixing bowl that has been warmed in the microwave, empty, for 1 minute.

Add yeast, milk, and water to the bowl, and let the yeast bloom for 15 minutes in a warm place. When the mixture looks frothy, it's ready.

Add flour, eggs, butter, sugar, and salt. (You can use a stand mixer outfitted with a dough hook for this step, or knead by hand on a floured surface for 5 minutes.)

Put your dough back in the bowl, cover with plastic wrap, and place back in a warm spot to rise for 30 minutes.

Ask an adult to help you with the frying. You can use a deep fat fryer or heat a deep skillet filled with 2 inches of oil. Oil should be between 350°F and 365°F (177°C and 185°C). (Check this with a kitchen thermometer.)

When the oil is at the right temperature, roll a tablespoonful of your dough between your hands to make a ball and lower gently into the oil.

Fry until golden brown. Sprinkle with sugar and serve.

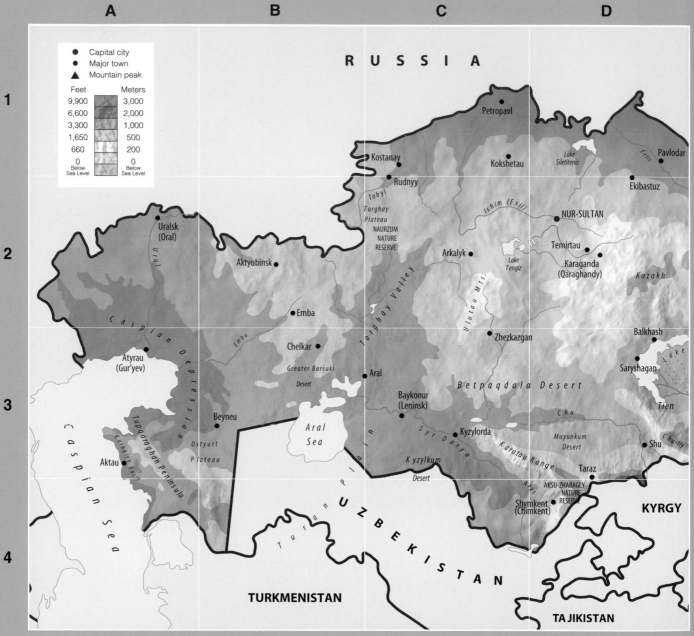

MAP OF KAZAKHSTAN

E

ZSTAN

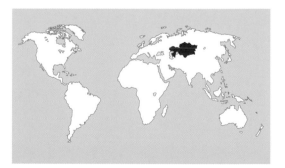

ECONOMIC KAZAKHSTAN

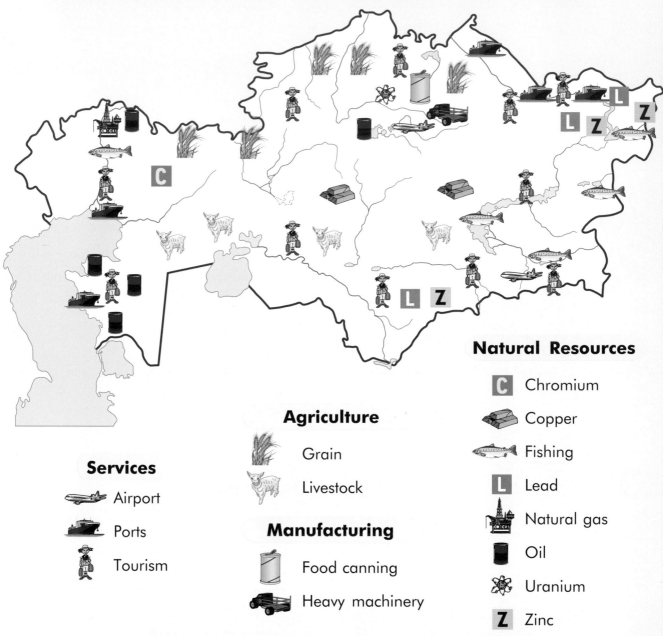

Services
- ✈ Airport
- 🚢 Ports
- 🧳 Tourism

Agriculture
- Grain
- Livestock

Manufacturing
- Food canning
- Heavy machinery

Natural Resources
- **C** Chromium
- Copper
- Fishing
- **L** Lead
- Natural gas
- Oil
- Uranium
- **Z** Zinc

ABOUT THE ECONOMY

All statistics are 2017 estimates unless otherwise stated.

OVERVIEW

After the USSR dissolved, Kazakhstan's economy suffered a decline. The country has since seen vast improvements, with its extensive fossil fuel reserves and mineral wealth being the engines making its economy work in the 21st century. Despite this, Kazakhstan is cautious in depending on fossil fuels and continues to work to diversify its economy. Agriculture remains important, especially livestock and grain production. Since joining the Eurasian Economic Union in 2010 (under its previous iteration, the Customs Union), more import and export opportunities have arisen, especially between Kazakhstan and its fellow union countries.

GROSS DOMESTIC PRODUCT (GDP)
$478.6 billion

CURRENCY
Tenge (KZT)
$1 = 389.71 KZT (2019 estimate)

INFLATION RATE
7.4 percent

LABOR FORCE
8.97 million

LABOR FORCE BY FIELD
agriculture: 18.1 percent
industry: 20.4 percent
services: 61.6 percent

UNEMPLOYMENT RATE
5 percent

AGRICULTURE
grain (mostly spring wheat and barley), potatoes, vegetables, melon, livestock

NATURAL RESOURCES
major deposits of petroleum, natural gas, coal, iron ore, manganese, chrome ore, nickel, cobalt, copper, molybdenum, lead, zinc, bauxite, gold, uranium

MAIN INDUSTRIES
oil, coal, iron ore, manganese, chromite, lead, zinc, copper, titanium, bauxite, gold, silver, phosphates, sulfur, uranium, iron and steel; tractors and other agricultural machinery; electric motors; construction materials

MAIN IMPORTS
machinery and equipment, metal products, foodstuffs

MAIN EXPORTS
oil and oil products, ferrous metals, chemicals, machinery, grain, wool, meat, coal

MAJOR TRADING PARTNERS
Italy, China, Netherlands, Russia, Switzerland, France, Germany, United States

CULTURAL KAZAKHSTAN

Steppes of Kazakhstan

The steppes stretch for more than 1,250 miles (2,000 km) from the Caspian Depression in the west to the Altai Mountains in the east. It is the largest dry steppe region in the world and can be likened to the North American prairies. This is an area of tremendous natural beauty, filled with lakes, hills, and forests. In the late 1950s, much of this land was plowed under and turned into wheat fields by hundreds of Russian and Ukrainian settlers during the Soviet Virgin Lands policy. Among the animals of the steppes are saiga antelope, corsac foxes, and steppe marmots.

Naurzum Nature Reserve

This second-oldest reserve in Kazakhstan covers over 215,000 acres (87,000 ha) south of the town of Kostanay, in the Kostanay region in the north. Created to protect the unique landscape of steppes, large lake systems, and forests, the reserve is an important migration stop for the Siberian crane. Rare white herons, jack-bustards, hisser swans, and grave eagles all find sanctuary here.

Lake Balkhash

One of the largest lakes in the world, the unique quality of this lake is that it contains half salt water and half fresh water.

Semipalatinsk Test Site

West of the town of Semey, this is the site where hundreds of nuclear bomb tests were conducted in the period between 1949 and 1991.

Altyn-Emel National Park

Spreading through the Almaty region, the park was founded in 1961 and is especially known for a natural phenomenon called sand barkhans. These sand dunes emit a singing sound when the wind blows.

Baykonur Cosmodrome

This space launch facility was built by the Soviets in the 1950s for their ambitious space program. It was from this facility that the world's first cosmonaut, Yuri Gagarin, was launched into space on April 12, 1961. The Cosmodrome is still in operation.

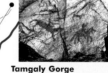

Tamgaly Gorge

In addition to the petroglyphs found in the Chu-Ily Mountains, this gorge also contains rock carvings, ancient settlements, and burial sites dating back to the Bronze Age.

Panfilov Park and Ascension Cathedral

This memorial park in Almaty was created to commemorate the 28 Kazakh soldiers who died fighting Nazi tanks in a village outside Moscow in 1941. Also in the park is Ascension Cathedral, built in 1907, a large wooden church built without using a single nail. During Soviet times, it was turned into a concert hall and museum. Today, it has regained use as a house of worship.

Karagiye Depression

At 433 feet (132 m) below sea level, this is one of the lowest points in the world. The landscape is rocky desert land and drifting sands. The 12th- to 14th-century Shakpak-Ata Mosque, hewn out of rock, is an attraction of this area.

Mausoleum of Khoja Ahmed Yasawi

Located in Turkistan, 102 miles (165 km) northwest of Shymkent in the Syr-Darya valley, this is an old site with great historical and religious significance. Khoja Ahmed Yasawi was the first great Turkic Muslim holy man, Sufi teacher, and mystical poet. He had tremendous influence in the Turkic-speaking world. The mausoleum was built by Timur, the 14th-century conqueror.

Aksu-Zhabagly Nature Reserve

Located in southern Kazakhstan, at the western extremity of the Western Tien Shan Mountains, this UNESCO World Heritage area is home to hundreds of species of birds, animals, and plants. It covers a variety of landscapes, from the dry semidesert to steppes, forests, and alpine meadows. It is honored as the home of the tulip.

Tien Shan

This mountain range stretches across more than 930 miles (1,500 km). It includes the highest peak in Kazakhstan, Khan-Tengri Peak (22,949 feet/6,995 m), known for the beautiful white, marble-like countenance that it presents. It anchors the southeast corner of the country.

ABOUT THE CULTURE

All figures are 2018 estimates unless otherwise noted.

OFFICIAL NAME
Republic of Kazakhstan

DESCRIPTION OF FLAG
sky-blue background with a gold sun with 32 rays above a golden eagle in the center; the hoist side of the flag has a yellow design called a "national ornamentation"

TOTAL AREA
1,052,090 square miles (2,724,900 sq km)

CLIMATE
continental; cold winters and hot summers, arid and semiarid

CAPITAL
Nur-Sultan

POPULATION
18,744,548

GOVERNMENT
republic; authoritarian presidential rule, with little power outside the executive branch

LIFE EXPECTANCY
total population: 71.4 years
male: 66.2 years
female: 76.3 years

BIRTH RATE
17.5 births per 1,000 population

DEATH RATE
8.2 deaths per 1,000 population

LITERACY RATE
99.8 percent (2015 estimate)

MAJOR RELIGIONS
Muslim 70.2 percent, Christian 26.2 percent, other 0.2 percent, atheist 2.8 percent, unspecified 0.5 percent (2009 estimate)

ETHNIC GROUPS
Kazakh 68 percent, Russian 19.3 percent, Uzbek 3.2 percent, Ukrainian 1.5 percent, Uighur 1.5 percent, Tatar 1.1 percent, German 1 percent, other 4.4 percent (2019 estimate)

MAIN LANGUAGES
Kazakh spoken by 83.1 percent (2017 estimate); Russian spoken by 94.4 percent (2009 estimate)

TIMELINE

IN KAZAKHSTAN	IN THE WORLD
1st century CE Central Asia is settled by Turkic-speaking and Mongol tribes.	
	ca. 570 Muhammad, the founder of Islam, is born in Mecca, Saudi Arabia.
8th–9th centuries Parts of southern Kazakhstan are conquered by Arabs. Arabs introduce Islam into the area.	
11th–12th centuries Tribal powers fight among themselves for control of the area.	
1219–1224 Genghis Khan and his Mongol tribes invade Kazakhstan and Central Asia.	**1347** The Black Death, also called the bubonic plague, begins killing millions of people in Europe.
15th century Kazakhs emerge as a recognizable group.	
	1530 The transatlantic slave trade, organized by the Portuguese in Africa, begins.
17th century Kazakhstan comes under the control of three tribal federations: the Great Horde, Middle Horde, and Lesser Horde.	**1620** Pilgrims sail the *Mayflower* to America.
1645 Russians set up an outpost on the north coast of the Caspian Sea.	
18th–19th century Russians are in firm control of the Kazakh tribes.	**1789–1799** The French Revolution takes place.
19th century The three hordes are abolished; Russian military rule is established.	
1837 Revolts against Russian rule begin.	
1906–1912 Thousands of Russian and Ukrainian farmers settle the land.	**1914–1918** World War I occurs.
1916 Kazakhs resist Russian attempt to recruit them in the fight against Germany.	**1917** Civil war breaks out in Russia following the Bolshevik Revolution.
1920 Kazakhstan becomes an autonomous republic of the USSR.	

IN KAZAKHSTAN	IN THE WORLD
1936	
Kazakhstan becomes a Soviet republic.	**1939–1945**
1940s	World War II occurs.
Forced resettlements to Kazakhstan of Koreans, Crimean Tatars, Germans, and others occur.	
1949	
The first nuclear test explosion is conducted at Semipalatinsk.	
1954	
The Virgin Lands policy begins.	
1957	
The Russians launch *Sputnik 1*, the world's first artificial satellite, from the Baykonur facility.	**1966** The Chinese Cultural Revolution begins.
1985	
Dinmukhamed Kunayev resigns as leader of the Communist Party of Kazakhstan (CPK).	
1989	
Nursultan Nazarbayev is made head of the CPK.	
1991	**1991**
Kazakhstan declares independence and joins the Commonwealth of Independent States.	Breakup of the Soviet Union takes place.
1993	
A new constitution is adopted.	
1997	
The capital of Kazakhstan is moved from Almaty to Akmola. Later, Akmola is renamed Astana.	**2001** Terrorists attack the United States on September 11.
2009	**2009**
The Kazakh section of a natural gas pipeline linking the country to China is unveiled.	Barack Obama becomes the first African American president of the United States.
	2016 Donald Trump is elected president of the United States.
2017	**2018**
President Nazarbayev calls for a change to the Kazakh language from using the Cyrillic alphabet to the Latin one.	Vladimir Putin wins Russian election and is sworn in to another six years as Russia's president.
2019	
Nazarbayev steps down, and Kassym-Jomart Tokayev becomes president. The capital city is renamed again, from Astana to Nur-Sultan.	

GLOSSARY

akyn (A-keen)
A Kazakh folk singer or storyteller.

horde
An ancient clan or group of nomadic Central Asian people who claim hunting and grazing rights over an area.

intelligentsia
A group of educated people forming a distinct social class in society.

jhyrau (JAI-rau)
A Kazakh lyric poet.

khan
The ruler of a Central Asian tribe.

nomad
A person who travels from place to place in a seasonal pattern to give their animals grazing grounds.

Politburo
The main political and executive committee of the Communist Party in the Soviet Union.

propaganda
Pamphlets, advertisements, or other communication methods that promote a cause or government in a favorable light.

protest
To stand up for a belief or tradition, usually through marches, public demonstration, or rallies.

shaman
A person who is believed to have the power to cure the sick, tell the future, and act as an intermediary between the people and the spirits.

Slav
A member of an ethnic and linguistic group of people in Eastern Europe—for example, Russians, Ukrainians, and Belarusians.

steppes
Vast and grassy plains found in parts of Europe, Asia, and the United States.

Turkic
A family of languages found in Eastern Europe and North and Central Asia, and a term to describe the people who speak these languages.

Union of Soviet Socialist Republics (USSR)
Also called the Soviet Union, the USSR was established as a result of the 1917 Russian Revolution. From 1940 to 1990, it consisted of 15 European and Asian republics. It broke up in 1991.

yurt
A dome-shaped felt tent used by nomads.

FOR FURTHER INFORMATION

BOOKS

Aitken, Jonathan. *Nazarbayev and the Making of Kazakhstan: From Communism to Capitalism.* London, UK: Continuum Pub Group, 2010.

Lillis, Joanna. *Dark Shadows: Inside the Secret World of Kazakhstan.* London, UK: I. B. Tauris, 2018.

Olcott, Martha Brill. *Kazakhstan: Unfulfilled Promise.* Washington, DC: Carnegie Endowment for International Peace, 2010.

Wight, Robert. *Vanished Khans and Empty Steppes: A History of Kazakhstan from Pre-History to Post-Independence.* London, UK: Silk Road Media, 2015.

WEBSITES

Astana Times. astanatimes.com.

CIA. *The World Factbook.* "Kazakhstan." https://www.cia.gov/library/publications/resources/the-world-factbook/geos/kz.html.

US Department of State Travel Advisory. https://travel.state.gov/content/travel/en/traveladvisories/traveladvisories/kazakhstan-travel-advisory.html.

FILMS

The Old Man. Directed by Ermek Tursunov, Kazakhfilm Studios, 2012.

Tulpan. Directed by Sergei Dvortsevoy, Zeitgeist Films, 2009.

MUSIC

Ninety-One. *Qarangy Zharyq*, JUZ Entertainment, 2017.

Various. *Dombra from Kazakhstan, Volume 2.* Buda Records, 2010.

Various. *Kazakhstan: Music from Almati.* Gallo, 1996.

BIBLIOGRAPHY

CIA. *The World Factbook*. "Kazakhstan." https://www.cia.gov/library/publications/resources/the-world-factbook/geos/kz.html.

"Embassy of the Republic of Kazakhstan." https://kazakhembus.com.

Helou, Anissa. *Feast: Food of the Islamic World*. New York, NY: Ecco Press, 2018.

"Kazakhstan." BBC. https://www.bbc.com/news/topics/c008ql15dl7t/kazakhstan.

"Kazakhstan Oil and Gas." https://www.export.gov/article?id=Kazakhstan-Oil-and-Gas.

"Kazakhstan Travel Advisory." US Department of State. https://travel.state.gov/content/travel/en/traveladvisories/traveladvisories/kazakhstan-travel-advisory.html.

Kindler, Robert. *Stalin's Nomads: Power and Famine in Kazakhstan*. Pittsburgh, PA: University of Pittsburgh Press, 2018.

Morris, Hugh. "19 Things You Didn't Know About Kazakhstan." *Telegraph*, December 15, 2015. https://www.telegraph.co.uk/travel/destinations/asia/kazakhstan/articles/Amazing-things-you-didnt-know-about-Kazakhstan.

"Official Information Source of the Prime Minister of the Republic of Kazakhstan." https://www.government.kz/en.

"Parliament of the Republic of Kazakhstan." http://www.parlam.kz/en.

INDEX

INDEX